"Powerful! That's the first word that ⟨...⟩ reading this excellent book. You will be inspired to make changes in your life."

—**Chandler Gerber**, featured in the film
From One Second to the Next

"Powerful. Life-changing insights shared simply. *The Heart of the Amish* can change your life for the better! Suzanne Woods Fisher's stories of the Amish will arm you with tools to forgive and find the path to reconciliation as they draw you closer to God."

—**Elizabeth B. Brown**, author, *Living Successfully with Screwed-Up People*

Praise for *Amish Peace*

"Fisher plants the reader inside Amish living rooms, barns, kitchens, and schoolhouses while distilling the best of what Plain life has to offer. Heartening and helpful."

—**Erik Wesner**, author, *Success Made Simple: An Inside Look at Why Amish Businesses Thrive* and the *Amish America* blog

"Suzanne has captured the calm spirit of the Amish community. She offers us a glimpse into a world of peace, serenity, and total commitment to family and God. This book just might change the way you live your life."

—**Glenda Lehman Ervin**, vice president, marketing, Lehman's

"As one who has experienced peace firsthand from a wonderful Amish family, I see the recent flurry of writing about the Amish as welcome to our hurting nation. Read *Amish Peace* and you will not only learn about this unique subculture, but you will also be inspired to live a life of peace."

—**Joel Kime**, pastor, Faith Church, Lancaster, PA

THE
HEART
OF THE
AMISH

Books by Suzanne Woods Fisher

Amish Peace:
Simple Wisdom for a Complicated World

Amish Proverbs:
Words of Wisdom from the Simple Life

Amish Values for Your Family:
What We Can Learn from the Simple Life

The Heart of the Amish:
Life Lessons on Peacemaking and the Power of Forgiveness

A Lancaster County Christmas

Christmas at Rose Hill Farm

Anna's Crossing

LANCASTER COUNTY
SECRETS

The Choice

The Waiting

The Search

THE INN AT
EAGLE HILL

The Letters

The Calling

The Revealing

STONEY RIDGE
SEASONS

The Keeper

The Haven

The Lesson

THE ADVENTURES
OF LILY LAPP
(WITH MARY ANN
KINSINGER)

Life with Lily

A New Home for Lily

A Big Year for Lily

A Surprise for Lily

THE
HEART
OF THE
AMISH

Life Lessons on Peacemaking
and the Power of Forgiveness

SUZANNE
WOODS
FISHER

a division of Baker Publishing Group
Grand Rapids, Michigan

Published by Revell
a division of Baker Publishing Group
P.O. Box 6287, Grand Rapids, MI 49516-6287
www.revellbooks.com

Printed in the United States of America

Library of Congress Cataloging-in-Publication Data is on file at the Library of Congress, Washington, DC.

ISBN 978-0-8007-2203-6

Unless otherwise indicated, Scripture quotations are from the Holy Bible, New International Version®. NIV®. Copyright © 1973, 1978, 1984, 2011 by Biblica, Inc.™ Used by permission of Zondervan. All rights reserved worldwide. www.zondervan.com

Scripture quotations labeled KJV are from the King James Version of the Bible.

Scripture quotations labeled Message are from *The Message* by Eugene H. Peterson, copyright © 1993, 1994, 1995, 2000, 2001, 2002. Used by permission of NavPress Publishing Group. All rights reserved.

To protect the privacy of those who have shared their stories with the author, some names and details have been changed. Permissions are on file for use of excerpts from the author's interviews with the identified and anonymous persons in this book.

Published in association with Joyce Hart of the Hartline Literary Agency, LLC

15 16 17 18 19 20 21   7 6 5 4 3 2 1

For those who need forgiveness
and those who need to forgive.
Lord, have mercy on us.

Contents

Contents

Acknowledgments

The idea for this book began after I had a radio interview with Becki Reiser (see "Through My Tears"). Her story touched me deeply and profoundly, partly, I think, because I have a daughter the same age as Becki's daughter, Liz. Mostly, I was stunned by the ability of Becki and her husband, Jeff, to make a choice to forgive at a crucial moment. In a way, they saved their family in that moment. The Reisers weren't Amish, but their response was very similar to the Amish of Nickel Mines: startling, radical forgiveness that set healing and wholeness into motion for those who had been deeply wounded.

And that's what started this journey of studying forgiveness for me.

Many Plain People shared their stories with me, for which I'm very grateful and without whom this book could not have been written. Individuals like Linda Yoder, who sent me regular leads to articles she thought I might find useful. And they were! Others like Mina Benedict, Sherry Gore, Sabine Aschmann, Joanne Hess Siegrist, Wilma Derksen, Terri Roberts, Chandler Gerber, Marie Roberts Monville, Dwight

LeFever, Jonas and Anne Beiler, and the many others who chose to remain anonymous. In most cases, identifying details have been changed to ensure the privacy of those involved. If the surname is an initial, such as Sarah Z., it is a pseudonym to protect privacy. Because of the emphasis that the Amish place on humility, the Amish people I interviewed were willing to share their stories but did not want their names to appear in print.

Another thank-you goes to my editor, Andrea Doering, who helped shape this book and bring it to life. The Revell team, of course, who take in a manuscript and turn out a polished book, ready for the market. Michele, Robin, Twila, Barb, and so many others whose hands touch a book in process. To Joyce Hart, my agent, who has been such a faithful supporter. To Lindsey Ciraulo, my crackerjack first reader. To my family, for listening and reacting to stories. Even—maybe, especially—when they gave me a blank look and suggested I skip a story or two.

My goal has been to present true stories of the Amish in a way that honors their heritage and inspires readers to live better lives. If there are any blunders, they are mine. If there is any takeaway value from this book into your life, consider it a gift from the example of the Amish.

Introduction

A warning: there's a pretty good chance you won't feel like the same person after reading this book. About halfway through the research and writing of this manuscript, I called my editor, Andrea. "If one more event occurs in my life that requires forgiveness, I will have to cancel this contract."

She just laughed.

"No, I'm not kidding!"

She laughed again.

Fine. She was no help. I got back to work.

The reason I started this book in the first place was because, as I have studied and written about the Amish, I have felt so impacted (*convicted* might be a better word) by their intentional forgiveness. The world got a taste of Amish grace after the school shooting at the Nickel Mines schoolhouse on October 2, 2006. The Amish responded with ready forgiveness, not vengeance, to the shooter's wife and family, because such a response has had centuries of conditioning. "When forgiveness arrived at the killer's home within hours of his crime," the authors of *Amish Grace* write, "it did not

13

appear out of nowhere. Rather, forgiveness is woven into the very fabric of Amish life, its sturdy threads having been spun from faith in God, scriptural mandates, and a history of persecution."[1]

The Amish believe that to forgive an enemy—so contrary to human nature—is to follow Jesus's instructions on forgiveness, as well as His example. And they don't just seek to forgive. They also love and bless those enemies.

I've always asserted that studying the Amish doesn't mean you have to "go Amish." But I've also discovered that much (not all, but much) of what drives their customs and traditions isn't, or shouldn't be, unique to the Amish. Many behaviors belong to all Christians. Key customs, such as the eternal significance of forgiving others, rest on verses from the Lord's Prayer, embedded in the Sermon on the Mount (Matt. 5–8). An oft-repeated proverb is "You can stop forgiving others when Christ stops forgiving you." The fundamentals of Amish forgiveness rest on a literal interpretation of this verse: "For if ye forgive men their trespasses, your heavenly Father will also forgive you: But if ye forgive not men their trespasses, neither will your Father forgive your trespasses" (Matt. 6:14–15 KJV).

Most Protestant traditions assert that forgiveness begins with God, that we receive it and *then* are able to forgive others. The Amish believe they receive forgiveness from God *only* if they extend forgiveness to others.

Better minds than mine have tried to settle that sticky theological debate. Anglican theologian John Stott might have best captured the intention of Jesus's words in his book *Through the Bible, Through the Year*: "This certainly does not mean that our forgiveness of others earns us the right to be forgiven. It is rather that God forgives only the penitent, and that one of the chief evidences of true penitence is a forgiving spirit."[2]

Whether, like the Amish, you accept a literal interpretation of those verses or a more figurative interpretation, it is clear that forgiving others who wrong us is evidence of the work of the Holy Spirit within us.

As I wrote and studied, it almost seemed as if this book conjured up opportunities to put into practice what I was writing about. Our family faced a serious issue with someone who has a volatile, unpredictable personality. During one particularly bad stretch, the person would email harsh accusations and then carry on with their day unaffected, while those of us who received their emails would feel, at best, distracted for the rest of the day. At worst, we'd be wiped out. My husband started calling those email missives "drive-by shootings."

My husband and I met with an insightful counselor a few times to sort out how to proceed with forgiveness. For our circumstances, we needed to know what it looked like to forgive someone who couldn't be trusted. Boundaries were necessary, but I also wanted to keep a door open for reconciliation. It took some time, but I could tell I had forgiven this individual when I genuinely celebrated good things that happened in their life. John Ortberg, pastor of Menlo Park Presbyterian Church, calls it "to will and work for good." I wanted the best for that person and could sincerely pray for God's blessings on them. I'm cautious about interactions with them, but I've learned how to keep a distance without being cold or unfeeling or dismissive. We're at a much better place than we were a year ago.

Other "opportunities" to practice forgiveness were less dramatic but strangely just as emotionally taxing. Not long ago, I got together with a friend, one of those persons who lacks a filter and requires a margin of grace. We chatted awhile, then out of the blue, she made a rude, hurtful comment about one of my children. I was stunned. I didn't even know how to respond. I could handle criticism from this friend about myself . . . but about one of my children? It cut to the core.

It has taken nearly as much effort to forgive my friend as it has to forgive our "email bomber." The Amish have a saying, "It isn't the mountains ahead that wear you out, it's the grain of sand in your shoes."

One thing for certain, my awareness of the need for forgiveness was growing. Giving it and receiving it. I want to be a person who makes forgiveness a way of life, a ready response. But how?

When it came to forgiving this friend for her hurtful remark about my child, I tried and tried to let it go. No luck. I knew her well enough to realize that if I were to say something to clear the air, she would dismiss it and say I was too sensitive.

A day came when I held out my hands, palms up, and said, "God, I just don't have it in me. Help me to forgive her."

An *aha* moment! I had been trying to forgive in my own power. In fact, most of the current literature about forgiveness is all about "choice." Choosing to forgive is a good start, but it won't get anyone to the finish line—the place of full forgiveness. It's holy work, forgiveness is. It's counterintuitive to our nature, yet so very essential to our well-being. We don't stand a chance at forgiving others without God's help.

I needed to learn how to lean on the grace of God. He wants us to fully forgive, to explore the truth of obtaining the grace of God (see Heb. 12:15). What a difference it made to invite God into the conversation! Forgiving this individual for her comment about my child didn't happen all at once, but it did happen.

The first stirring toward forgiveness began during one of my husband's business trips when I was alone for a couple weeks. It occurred to me how lonely this woman was. Unbidden, I started remembering kindnesses that she had done for my family. I sensed God was at work, helping me to put that comment in its proper perspective. It was a hurtful remark, but it wasn't symbolic of the entire relationship. I'm sure I've made plenty of careless and hurtful remarks too. Little by little, God replaced my indignation with understanding. As the process began, I felt something settle, deep inside, in a spiritual way. It wasn't long before the hurtful comment receded to the back of my mind and I knew I had fully forgiven her.

This book looks at the subject of forgiveness from many different angles, borrowing examples from the Amish and other Anabaptist groups. It's meant to be a book filled with takeaway value, insights, and suggestions for healing and wholeness that can be brought into your life.

The first section includes stories of forgiveness in day-to-day life, where most of our people problems lie. The stories in the second section might be the ones that stick with you long after reading this book. They are profound. You will see how only God could provide the ability to forgive in such circumstances. These stories flip the telescope.

What does it mean to "live forgiven"? It means we invite God into the friction of our daily situations even when they don't seem big enough, or dire enough. They're like a pebble in our shoe. Not irritating enough to take off our shoe and shake it out, but still, it's always there. Wearing, wearing, wearing.

The Amish practice forgiveness right from the start, modeling it to their children, turning negative thoughts into positive ones, being the first to extend the olive branch to others. Forgiveness is a habitual way of thinking. They believe that life *isn't* fair—the toast burns, the milk spills, the car breaks down. They believe we are part of an imperfect world, far from the Garden. They *expect* life not to be fair, so when the hard things come into their life—and they do, just like everyone's life—they've had experience with how to manage them.

What will spill out of you when you are under great stress is what spills out of you now in the day-to-day friction of living. Our ability to forgive what seems unforgiveable is deeply connected to how we handle the smaller transgressions: when someone cuts in front of us at the grocery store, when our spouse forgets an anniversary, when our family accidentally locks us out of the house.

The goal of this book is to help you make a habit of forgiving. None of us can know for sure where life will take us, but we do know there will be potholes and detours and fender benders along the way. We just don't have much control over the things that happen to us in life. To think that your life will be perfect and nothing will ever go wrong is a serious self-deception, writes Dr. Dick Tibbits, author of *Forgive to Live: How Forgiveness Can Save Your Life.*

> Since you know you will need to forgive someone in the future, why not practice forgiveness every chance you get? Each time you forgive, it becomes easier to forgive the next time. Forgiveness is like a muscle: the more it is exercised, the more it can do. And the more you practice forgiving the little hurts in life, the better you will be able to handle the big hurts.[3]

Dr. Martin Luther King Jr., who taught and lived forgiveness, said it best: "Forgiveness is not an occasional act; it is a permanent attitude."[4]

PART ONE

EVERYDAY FRICTION

The trouble with our past is that it refuses to stay past.

Amish proverb

Not long ago, a phone call came in from an Amish man who had seen an advertisement I placed in *The Budget* to seek out stories of forgiveness. This elderly fellow was blessed with the gift of conversation—he did the talking and I did the listening. He had some interesting thoughts to share, including a very relevant story about a time when his business had been taken advantage of by a customer.

He told me the story in exhaustive detail. At the end of our conversation, I asked him if he might be willing to let me use the story in this book. After all, wasn't that why he called?

"Absolutely not!" he roared back. "It's best not to remember these things. It's best not to dwell."

As I hung up, I couldn't stop grinning. Without meaning to, that Amish man—with a touch of irony—had summed up the Amish way of coming to grips with offenses and injustices. They might try to live separate from the world, but the world doesn't separate easily. They have their share of hurt feelings, committed wrongs, crimes against the innocent. But as a practice, they choose not to dwell on them, they don't give those things power over them or let them control their lives, including their thought life.

Threaded throughout many Amish sayings is the emphasis on taking the initiative to forgive, regardless of who is at fault.

- "He who cannot forgive breaks the bridge over which he himself must pass."
- "When someone hurts your feelings, it's unimportant unless you persist in remembering it."
- "The best way to get the last word in is to apologize."

These sayings show how the Amish aim the spotlight on the restorer of the relationship, not on the question of fault.

In the early years of our marriage, we lived in Houston, Texas. Because of Houston's hot and humid weather, the trash collectors picked up trash twice a week—on Mondays and Thursdays. Sometimes the truck would rumble down the street earlier in the morning than usual and we didn't get our garbage out in time for the pickup. By the time the next pickup day arrived, you can imagine how eager we were to get rid of the accumulated garbage. Who in their right mind would intentionally let trash get crammed full and backed up when there was a chance to get rid of it? Yet that's what we do when we nurse grudges, hold on to hurts, let anger fester, allow resentments and bitterness to brew—things that foul our life and spoil our relationships. We do with our memories, emotions, and relationships what we wouldn't do with rotten bananas and spoiled milk.

We refuse to let go of the garbage.

According to the Laboratory of Neuro Imaging at the University of Southern California, the average person has about 70,000 thoughts a day.[1] (Some research has put that number at 50,000 or less, but whether the number is 15,000, 50,000, or 70,000, what's important is those are *big* numbers.) Psychologist and Nobel Prize winner Daniel Kahneman determined that the "psychological present" is a window of about three seconds—everything else that runs through our minds is either past or future.[2] An old Penn Dutch proverb seemed to have already figured that out without the supporting data: "Regrets over yesterday and the fear of tomorrow are twin thieves that rob us of the moment."

With all that traffic running through our brains, shouldn't we make more of an effort to stop dwelling on negative thoughts, patterns, endless loops? Scripture has an antidote to holding on to mental garbage:

> Summing it all up, friends, I'd say you'll do best by filling your minds and meditating on things true, noble, reputable, authentic, compelling, gracious—the best, not the worst; the beautiful, not the ugly; things to praise, not things to curse. Put into practice what you learned from me, what you heard and saw and realized. Do that, and God, who makes

everything work together, will work you into his most excellent harmonies. (Phil. 4:8–9 Message)

Here's a favorite Amish saying that helps manage a returning negative reflection: "Thoughts might arrive for a visit, but you don't have to invite them to stay." Imagine yourself, on each of your garbage pickup days, putting out your emotional trash for God to haul away. In its place, ask Him to fill the open space with forgiveness.

And then ponder this: If you have 70,000 thoughts per day, you have 70,000 chances to do it better.

A Little Amish General Store

---

*If you won't admit you've been wrong, you love
yourself more than truth.*

Amish proverb

B link twice and you'll miss the little Amish general store
in Buchanan County, Iowa. It's tucked down a single-
lane dirt road, hidden behind a white farmhouse,
obvious only to those who know to look for it. Inside are
shelves filled with all kinds of humble necessities: enormous
black rubber men's galoshes, Band-Aids, Kingsford charcoal,
Mason jars. Lining the back of the store are shelves of glass
hurricanes, in all sizes. They're used to contain the flame of
kerosene lamps, common lighting in Amish homes. Above the
shelves of glass hurricanes is a handwritten sign, so startling
in its message that you have to read it twice:

*If You Break It, Please Let Us Know
So That We Can Forgive You.*

When asked about the sign, the Amish storekeeper smiled, her face so open and honest and sincere that one couldn't help but smile in return. "We know that accidents happen, that fragile things break. We'd rather be told something broke than have someone hide it or pretend it didn't happen. We expect a few problems now and then."

What an upside-down view of modern retailing! Most stores that display delicate or breakable items warn parents with small children and instill fear in the clumsy: "If you break it, you pay" or "You break it, you buy it." The message is clear: Shop at your own risk.

In a way, people have similar warning signs, though they're not always visible to the human eye. In fact, it would be much easier if they wore a sign around their neck that stated the obvious: "I'm fragile. I'm broken. I'm wounded. I had a difficult childhood. I'm sensitive. I'm unhappy. I'm angry. If you hurt me, you are going to have to pay for it."

But what would your response be to a friend who had a sign like the Amish store's over the door of her home? Imagine if it said something like this: "Hurts and mistakes and misunderstandings happen in all relationships. Our friendship is more important than allowing an issue to divide us. If there comes a time when you might hurt me, intentionally or otherwise, I'm prepared to offer you forgiveness. Just ask." Most likely, this is a friend you would visit often. You know you are loved. If your friendship hits a bump or two, as most do, it can be restored. Sociologist Brené Brown calls this kind of person a "stretch-mark friend." In *Daring Greatly*, she writes about such friendships: "Our connection has been stretched and pulled so much that it's become part of who we are, a second skin, and there are a few scars to prove it."[1]

What about you? What if you were to hang a similar sign declaring a generous spirit of forgiveness in your own home? "This is a family that allows a margin of error. Our love for each other is greater than our failures. If we say or do something we shouldn't have, forgiveness is always available. Just ask."

I imagine the sign over God's front door is even more generous and potent: "If you're broken, just let Me know. My Son died on the cross and rose again to offer you forgiveness for your sins."

If forgiveness is readily available, why is there a condition—asking—placed on these signs? Why do we have to ask at all? When we ask forgiveness of others—our friends, our spouse, our children, our neighbors, our colleagues—we admit our culpability, setting into motion the process of healing and restoring the relationship. When we ask God for forgiveness, we admit our sinfulness, properly posturing ourselves before a holy God (1 John 1:8–10).

But we can't receive if we don't ask. For that is the essence of God's story of forgiveness.

REFLECTIONS ON PEACEMAKING

How would your relationships be different if forgiveness were built into them? If you were a student of God's forgiving nature—that is, if forgiveness became a way of life—how would it transform your relationship with your family? Your friends? Your co-workers? Your neighbors?

Identify a few of your own shortcomings and weaknesses. What mistakes have you made that hurt others? Who has forgiven you for these mistakes? Who has been a "stretch-mark friend" to you?

The most difficult seven words to say can be the most healing to a relationship: "I was wrong. Will you forgive me?" What makes those seven words so potent?

Metaphorically speaking, what changes in your heart would have to take place to have a sign like the Amish general store's over your life?

 Plain _Truth_

As of 2014, a total of 290,090 Amish live in North America. With an average family size of six to eight children, the population doubles every twenty years. At that rate, by the year 2050, there will be over one million Amish.[2]

The Red Mutza

*There is no love without forgiveness, and no for-
giveness without love.*

Amish proverb

H ave you ever noticed that the color red is seldom
used by the Amish? Not in women's dresses, nor
men's shirts, nor children's clothing. Not even in
quilts. But it wasn't always that way.

Hundreds of years ago, a Mutza (frock coat) made of red
woven fabric was considered common for Amish men of
Germany to wear—but only to church. Most Amish men
have two kinds of coats, each with their own function. The
ordinary coat can be used for work, but after a young man
is baptized, the Mutza is always worn to preaching service.
This garment is longer than the ordinary work coat and has
a split tail. Think of it as a suit and tie, minus the matching
pants. And the tie.

As traditions developed in the Amish church, the color red became frowned upon, then forbidden. In the late part of the eighteenth century, Christian Hershberger was born and raised in Germany, joined the Amish church, and—like so many of his peers—emigrated to Pennsylvania as a single young man. One of the few things he brought with him from the Old World was his red Mutza. Eventually, Christian met and married Barbara P. Beachy of Somerset County, and they settled down in Holmes County, Ohio, to raise their family. He never wore the red Mutza to church, but he never got rid of it either.

Christian and Barbara had a son named Gabriel. After Gabriel grew up, was baptized, and got married, he wore the red Mutza to church. The red Mutza raised eyebrows among the Holmes County church, and a ruling was made that men's clothing should be black or dark blue. Definitely *not* red. The church decided that Gabriel's red Mutza could not be allowed.

Gabriel stood firm. It was his father's coat, he reasoned. A coat that had been worn among the Amish in Germany. A coat with history. He refused to put it away. The church stood firm and would not approve of a red coat for men. So there was a standoff.

Along came communion in the fall. A number of church members voiced their opinion that communion should not be held until Gabriel's red coat was put away. Gabriel refused to budge. The bishop, a man named Mose Miller, was a peacemaker, known for his patience and love, and he wanted no ill will between brother and brother. He asked the church to be more patient, to allow time for the matter to be peacefully settled, without putting pressure on Gabriel.

In October, Gabriel made it known to the church that he was planning to build a corncrib. In those days, buildings were built like Lincoln Logs, with cuttings of notched logs locking into place with another notched log. It was back-breaking work, doable only with help from neighbors. Then, as now, work frolics were formed among the Amish to help each other with large building projects.

But no one came to Gabriel's frolic. When the church members were asked to help build the corncrib, they refused to help him. Gabriel wasn't at peace with the church, they pointed out, all because of that red Mutza.

Bishop Mose, a carpenter, lived about two miles away from the Hershberger farm. When he realized that Gabriel would be working alone on the corncrib, he said, "It will not do to be revengeful. We must win people in love and not with hate."

So Bishop Mose left his work unfinished, hitched his horse to a hack, and took his carpenter tools along to help Gabriel. With high scaffolding, a rope, block, and tackle, the two men pulled each log up to set it into place. Bishop Mose worked side by side with Gabriel for three full days, without any help from other church members. He never said a word about the red Mutza or about the festering troubles with the church members or about delaying communion. He just worked alongside Gabriel, as his friend and neighbor.

At the end of the third day, the walls were up, ready for the roof. Gabriel told Bishop Mose that he could manage putting on the roof by himself. Raising the walls had been the hardest part.

So Bishop Mose brought his horse out of Gabriel's barn to hitch to the hack, ready to get home to the work that was waiting for him. Gabriel helped him hitch up and thanked him for his help over the last three days.

As Mose was about to climb onto his hack, Gabriel stopped him by putting a hand on his shoulder. "I will put that red coat away for good, and come offer peace and love to the church next Sunday. I will not wear that coat again, as an honor to the church."[1]

The old people of Holmes County often spoke of Bishop Mose's example of patient loving-kindness. He won Gabriel over, they said, without one word about his red coat. This, they point out, is what love, rather than revenge, can do to win people as peaceful friends. Some even wonder what might have been set into motion among the Amish in Holmes County had Bishop Mose tried to win Gabriel over by force, rather than by love.

"Peace is worth our greatest effort," Ken Sande writes in *Resolving Everyday Conflict*.[2] The Bible tells us that we should "make every effort to keep the unity of the Spirit through the bond of peace" (Eph. 4:3). The Greek word in this verse that is translated "make every effort" means to strive eagerly . . . earnestly . . . diligently. It's a word that a trainer of gladiators might have used when he sent men to fight to the death in the Coliseum. "Make every effort to stay alive today!" Peace is worth that life-and-death effort. If we want to enter into all the peace God has for us, we have to give it our all.

We have to give it our red Mutza.

 REFLECTIONS ON PEACEMAKING

Why is it so hard for us to admit our part in causing a conflict?

How is this story—in which Bishop Mose never even mentions the "hot topic" of the red Mutza but instead comes alongside Gabriel to help him—an excellent example of resolving a conflict?

What damaging results have you seen from conflict? What good results could you enjoy by working toward peace?

Consider the red coat to be a metaphor for change. How will you respond if your daughter comes home from college with a tattoo on her ankle? Or a new neighbor moves in next door and keeps her creepy Halloween decorations up through Christmas? The lesson of Bishop Mose is to see past the offense to offer grace to the person. Who, in your immediate circle, do you disapprove of? What act of grace can you take to get past your disapproval to connect to the individual in a loving way?

Is there a "red coat" in your life that you're holding on to, just because you can? Something that is well within your rights, but it might be offensive to another?

 Plain *Truth*

In Amish society, styles of dress are important as symbols of unity and community. "All these garments," John Hostetler writes in *Amish Society*, "were common in Europe among the rural people." While such style of clothing was once very ordinary among peasants, the Amish have retained them as a symbolic way of life. Whether as a language of "protest" or as custom, Amish patterns of dress form a strong basis of identity and exclusion. Like all boundary mechanisms, dress serves to keep the insider separate from the world and to identify the outsider.[3]

An Olive Branch
of Juicy Fruit Gum

Forgiveness can straighten what failures have made crooked.

Amish proverb

Mary-Ann Kirkby grew up in a Hutterite Colony in Canada. The Hutterites, started by Jakob Hutter in 1536, are post-Reformation Anabaptists and hold many core values and beliefs with their Plain cousins—with one significant exception: the Hutterites share all property in common.

Like most Hutterite children, Mary-Ann had a happy, secure childhood. When she was ten years old, she spent hours playing with her best friend, Sandra, on a huge mound of sand near the houses. "There, we created our future, the layout of the bedrooms, our kitchenettes and living rooms. Using toothpicks, we created our family. A full-length toothpick represented the mother (Sandra and I) and the father, our fabulous future husbands. The rest of the toothpicks were broken down in size to represent the ages of our children. I always insisted I would have four children: two boys and two girls."

Sandra and Mary-Ann worked side by side, playing with this imaginary toothpick family. "The arguments started when it came to describing our children. Sandra would be rather straightforward and predictable in her descriptions. But when it was time for my turn, I went totally fairy tale. I described one of my imaginary daughters looking like Rapunzel, with long hair flowing down her back. Her hair was so blond and shiny and beautiful it made people gasp. By the time I finished my elaborate descriptions, poor Sandra realized she needed to dust her little family off and make them seem a bit more spiffy. She would start to steal my lines. This really made my blood boil. In my opinion, this was pure plagiarism, and I let her have it. And she gave as good as she got."

Mary-Ann said that both girls were sometimes referred to as "hot pots" because they had a tendency, on the "mad chart," to go from zero to ten. "Sometime during our shouting matches, one or the other of us would storm off." The standoff would last for a few days. Neither girl would give an inch.

After a couple of days of not speaking, one or the other—usually the guiltier party—showed up at the door of the other holding up a stick of Juicy Fruit gum. "Juicy Fruit gum was treasured," Mary-Ann said. "It was a favorite item in our colony and came to represent something special. If the gum was accepted, then the matter was behind us and never spoken of again. If the gum wasn't accepted, then we gave each other a couple more days to pout and then tried again, usually with better success. 'I'm sorry' wasn't a part of our vocabulary . . . it was just something I accepted as fact as soon as Sandra accepted my gum."

As a habit, Mary-Ann did not discuss their squabbles with anyone, not even her mother. "Mom would surely have tried to minimize their importance, and I wanted to be mad. The toothpick game was important to me, and I felt very justified." But not so justified that she didn't want to reconcile the squabble with Sandra. Well, when she was good and ready.

"I think we need a lot more Juicy Fruit in our lives," Mary-Ann said. "It's about giving each other time and space to realize . . . it's not worth it. I love and miss this person and I'm going over there to patch it up."

 ## Reflections on Peacemaking

For those two little Hutterite girls, a stick of Juicy Fruit was their version of an olive branch, as good as an apology. It was their way to make an effort toward bridging the dam, toward reconciliation. For adults, flowers are often used as olive branches. Words, though, are best of all. When you were a child, how did you make things right with a friend? How do you do it as an adult?

Apologies can be hard to make because it takes a spirit of humility to admit mistakes, which doesn't come naturally. Define humility and explain its connection to forgiveness. Why is humility a sign of strength, not weakness?

Is it possible to forgive when we still feel hurt or angry? Why or why not?

If you decide to forgive someone who has offended you, how will you show that you really mean it?

Apologies are frequently needed in relationships. Jesus instructed His followers to make things right with those we've offended (Matt. 5:23–24; 18:15–20). And the apostle Paul said, "If it is possible, as far as it depends on you, live at peace with everyone" (Rom. 12:18). Living at peace may require apologies. But taking responsibility for one's part in a conflict can bring healing and restoration to a relationship. We all mess up with those we love. Swallow your pride and make the first move.

 ## Plain *Truth*

The Hutterites share the same Anabaptist roots as the Amish and Mennonites, and stem from the Radical Reformation period. They maintain a plain form of dress and live lives heavily shaped by their Christian faith, including pacifism. There are some key differences between Hutterites, Amish, and plain Mennonites. Hutterites live communally, on colonies, sharing all their worldly goods, and they use modern technology. Today, there are about 42,000 Hutterites living primarily in North America—Canada and the upper Midwest. To learn more about Hutterites, go to www.hutterites.org.

A Jar of Pickles

It is better to fill a little place right than a big place wrong.

Amish proverb

Yoder's Country Cupboard is a local store that is tucked into the back of Vernon Yoder's property. Eight years ago, Vernon, his wife, and four daughters had moved from Ohio to western New York to join an expanding Amish community. The store quickly established itself and developed a reputation for customer service. It provided a place for locals to buy deli meat, cheese, bulk foods, spices, candy, and more. Campers from Lake Ontario, five miles away, find it a convenient place to restock their food supply.

One day, a middle-aged woman stomped into Yoder's Country Cupboard and slapped a glass jar of dill spears down on the checkout counter. "These pickles are awful," she said in a loud voice. "They're all mushy. I want my money back."

Vernon Yoder picked up the jar of pickles. It wasn't a brand of pickles he carried at the store. "Sure, we can give you your money back, but it might interest you to know that we never sold that type of pickles."

"Oh, I got them here all right." The woman strode to the cooler. "Right here on this shelf." Not seeing any other jars with that brand label, she added, "Must be you're sold out of them right now."

Slightly red-faced, the woman returned to the checkout counter with her palm splayed open, waiting for her refund. Rachel, the young woman who was working the cash register, looked at Vernon, eyebrows raised in a question. Vernon glanced at the price sticker: $4.26. He gave a quick nod and Rachel handed over the money.

"Thanks." The woman headed out the door, flip-flops thwacking on the tile.

It's easy to think of all the reasons Vernon shouldn't have given the woman her money. But that's not the way Vernon Yoder or most Amish would view the situation. To Vernon, giving $4.26 to the customer was a small price to pay for keeping the peace. He believed that turning the other cheek to a customer paved the way for reconciliation, and he was known as a man who would go the second mile for his customers. By not responding in a defensive way, he could remain on friendly terms with such a customer in the future. And that became evident with the pickle jar lady.

The following day, the woman in flip-flops came back into Yoder's Country Cupboard. "It all came back to me," she said with a sheepish look. "I got those pickles at Kirby's Farm Market. Not here." She flipped a five-dollar bill onto the counter and said, "I'm very sorry."

Reflections on Peacemaking

Much of the success of stores like Yoder's Country Cupboard has to do with the way the shop owners provide service to their customers. Each customer is considered to be a long-term relationship. "The discretion of a man deferreth his anger; and it is his glory to pass over a transgression" (Prov. 19:11 KJV). What changes when you start thinking of the people who come across your path as long-term relationships?

"Working toward peaceful solutions to conflict isn't our natural human response," writes Ken Sande in *Resolving Everyday Conflict*. "Some people see conflict as a hazard that threatens to sweep them off their feet and leave them bruised and hurting, so they react by making every attempt to escape the situation. Others see conflict as an obstacle to be conquered quickly and completely, even if they hurt others in the process."[1] What is your usual response to conflict—escape or attack? Most of us jump between the extremes.

Think of a time you responded defensively to someone who wronged you. And then think of a time when you showed grace. What were the consequences to the relationships for each response? Which response brought a healthy and restored relationship?

Plain *Truth*

While Amish do not serve in law enforcement, and view use of force as wrong, they nevertheless do rely on police protection and are grateful to those who do the work to provide them with a safe environment in which to live. Amish beliefs on law enforcement and litigation are ultimately rooted in their founding belief of non-resistance, found in the Dordrecht Confession, and undergirded by their interpretation of Two Kingdoms Doctrine.[2]

Three Words a Mother Never Wants to Hear from Her Fifteen-Year-Old Daughter

A forgiving heart grows stronger with exercise.

Amish proverb

Sarah B. grew up in LaGrange County, Indiana, on a farm that her great-grandfather had once tilled. She is small and plump and must have worked about fifteen or sixteen hours that day, but she looked as fresh as a daisy. Her warmth was reassuring and welcoming, and her eyes grew soft as she spoke of her godly heritage. "My grandfather was a minister, my father was a bishop, my husband is a deacon."

Such a lineage means a great deal to her. "My sisters and me," she said, "we grew up knowing that we had to behave. People were watching." She was up to the task. Sarah married her childhood sweetheart at the age of eighteen and had her first child at nineteen. In due time, more children arrived. Life was sweet for Sarah.

And then everything turned upside down on a hot August afternoon when Sarah's firstborn, her fifteen-year-old daughter, whispered words no mother would ever want to hear: "Mom, I'm pregnant."

"That moment shook me to my core," Sarah said. "I didn't *want* my daughter to be pregnant. I didn't *want* to be a thirty-four-year-old grandmother. I didn't *want* my husband, a new deacon, to have a mess in his own family. I had tried my best to be a good mom. I felt humiliated. I was sure that everybody thought I had failed. I wanted to hide. I struggled with God. How could He have let this happen to me? I was a good girl. I did everything right."

For the first time in her life, Sarah said she became aware of how it felt to be wounded, to suffer, to feel broken. "I began to see my own judgmental tendencies, to realize how critical I had been of other people." Shame, she discovered, had been a very powerful tool to control others. "But when I *felt* shame, I was astounded at what it did to me. It made me feel stuck. All I could think about was my own failure, my shortcomings, my sins."

Over the next few months, Sarah found herself changing from the inside—areas, she said, that were necessary. "I grew compassionate to those around me who I knew were also suffering. Suddenly I wasn't judging them because I was right alongside them. I think I finally realized that we are all wounded, each in our way. That God can use our wounds for His purpose."

Sarah started to relate to people around her in a different way. "The closer I drew to Christ, the more empathy I developed for others. The more I loved the Lord, the more I loved those He loved." And that included having the grace to forgive her daughter, as well as the young man (non-Amish) who had fathered the child. "He did not want to marry our daughter, nor did we want him to," Sarah said, without malice. And that was all she had to say about the matter. Sarah and her husband are raising their little granddaughter, now a vivacious and charming seven-year-old, as part of their brood.

She admitted that this wasn't the path she would have ever wanted or expected for her family. "But would I change it? No, absolutely not. I'm a different person because of this experience. When someone else is facing a difficult situation, I'm able to say, 'Me too. This happened in our family too, and we got through it. No—better than that. We are better *because* of it.'"

Sociologist Brené Brown is a vulnerability researcher at the University of Houston. In one of the most watched talks on the TED.com website, Brown encouraged listeners to embrace their brokenness. "Vulnerability is not weakness. It's emotional risk. In order for us to have connection, we have to allow ourselves to be seen. Really seen. To be vulnerable, to let ourselves be seen, to be honest."[1]

One friend told Sarah that, during her family's hard time, they displayed God's splendor to the community. "Isn't that amazing?" Sarah said, smiling that radiant smile of hers, in which her whole face lights up. "To think that our trial could end up displaying God's splendor. Only God could do that."

 ## REFLECTIONS ON PEACEMAKING

Define *empathy*. Why does empathy have an essential connection to forgiveness?

Empathy, Sarah implied, was lacking in her life until she faced a personal hardship. In what way can someone who has walked a difficult path relate to others who suffer in a way that no other can?

What difficulty in your life has taught you empathy?

Sarah said she realized she had hurt others with her judgmental tendencies. What mistakes have you made that have hurt others? Who has forgiven you for these mistakes?

Sarah's friend gave her timely encouragement when she said that the way Sarah's family handled a teenager's unplanned pregnancy was used to display God's splendor. What do you think her friend saw in their family that made such an impression? Think of the difficulties in your life. How is God redeeming those difficulties so they can be used to display His splendor? (See Rom. 8:28.)

 Plain *Truth*

"Do the Amish have problems? Yes. They are humans and, like all human societies, have their share of problems. Sometimes rebellious youth act out and abuse alcohol or use drugs. Some marriages turn sour. There are documented cases of incest and sexual abuse in some families. Although such problems do exist, there are no systematic studies to enable comparisons with other groups or mainstream society. In general, the Amish way of life provides many sources of satisfaction for most of its members."[2]

Keeping Secrets

*Temptations are sure to ring your doorbell, but
it's your fault if you invite them home for dinner.*

Amish proverb

Andy K. is a big man with bushy eyebrows, well built for a curmudgeonly role. And yet he's surprisingly warm and speaks with disarming honesty, especially when you realize he is a sixty-year-old Amish man. He has struggled with a problem area in his life: pornography. He had first been exposed to pornography as a teenager, when he came across *Playboy* magazines thrown out in a dumpster behind a local gas station. "All the boys knew they were there. It was something we did on Saturday nights. Go check out the dumpster behind the station." He never knew to whom the magazines belonged, but they seemed to show up regularly in that dumpster.

When Andy became baptized as a church member, he went out of his way to avoid traveling the road that passed that gas

44

station and its tempting dumpster. "That worked for a while, but then I overheard a fellow talk about a phone number that was kind of interesting." Andy was installing kitchen cabinets in an English woman's home and found himself alone in the house one afternoon. He used the customer's phone to dial the number. It turned out to be a sex hotline. Andy said that one phone call was as powerful as throwing gas on smoldering coals. "All I could think about was looking for a chance to make the next call." Whenever he was out on a job, he would find a way to use the customer's phone. "It was wrong. I knew it, but I couldn't help it."

Troubled by guilt, Andy finally decided to confide in a close friend about his problem. "I asked this man to keep it confidential and to pray for me. He assured me he would, that he understood. Not twenty-four hours later, the leaders were paying me a call."

His friend had gone to the church leaders to report Andy's conduct. The bishop, the ministers, and the deacon acted with a swift hand. They told Andy to go to every customer, apologize, and make financial restitution for the phone calls he had made. And then he would be expected to confess his actions to the church at the next Members' Meeting.

"I was really furious with him," Andy said. "Really angry. For a long time, I blamed my friend. I lost a lot of repeat business from my customers. It caused a lot of problems at home—with my wife, with my family. I was viewed with less respect in the eyes of others. I felt like my friend betrayed me, like he should have been honest with me. I wished he would've let me try to handle this myself. That's why I told him about it in the first place. I knew I needed to stop doing it, but he didn't give me a chance. I wanted to get even with him, to make him hurt the way I was hurting."

A few months later, Andy attended the church's Gmay (Council Meeting Sunday), held two weeks before spring communion. "When the bishop told us to make things right with our neighbors, this friend's face popped into my mind. And let me tell you, I wrestled with God about it, the way Jacob wrestled with the angel. I didn't want to make things right with that man. I had refused to speak to him for the last few months. But I knew I had to give up my pride, my rights. I had to, if I wanted to take communion with a clean conscience."

Andy brought out his Bible and opened it up, pointing to a specific verse in which Jesus explained to the disciples about the urgency of reconciliation. "Therefore if thou bring thy gift to the altar, and there rememberest that thy brother hath ought against thee; Leave there thy gift before the altar, and go thy way; first be reconciled to thy brother, and then come and offer thy gift" (Matt. 5:23–24 KJV).

"Want to know when Jesus said I should go?" he said, drumming the Bible with his index finger. "Thirty days? One week? No. Jesus said to get up and leave the worship gathering. Crawl out over the long bench of people. The Bible says it's more important to fix that relationship than to continue worshiping and singing songs. Leave the worship gathering, go meet with your neighbor."

In *Resolving Everyday Conflict*, Ken Sande writes that taking responsibility for your part of a conflict is a crucial step toward peacemaking. "If I'm only 2 percent responsible for a conflict, I'm 100 percent responsible for that 2 percent. Confessing your fault to the person you offended is the way you fully own your part of a conflict."[1]

Andy took to heart the words of the Bible. He went to the man's farm and found him in the barn, feeding the horses. Silently, Andy helped him finish his chores, then the two leaned against the horse stalls—one on each side of the aisle—and started to talk, tentatively at first, then more openly. "He said he left me that day and didn't feel right about keeping this to himself, that he didn't feel right with me thinking I could solve my problem all by myself. He thought I was trying to bury my behavior, to keep it hidden, and that would only bring more problems in the long run. He said we belong to a community, and when one of us sins, it affects everyone, like the way a flu bug runs through the church. He was trying to act out of love, not ill will. That meant a lot to me, to hear him say that."

The church, to the Amish, is not just a worshiping community but also a redemptive community. The act of confession is integral to restoring individuals to full fellowship—with God and man.

In his book *Life Together*, Dietrich Bonhoeffer wrote:

> In confession the break-through to community takes place. Sin demands to have a man by himself. It withdraws him from the community. The more isolated a person is, the more destructive will be the power of sin over him, and the more deeply he becomes involved in it, the more disastrous is his isolation. Sin wants to remain unknown. It shuns the light. In the darkness of the unexpressed it poisons the whole being of a person. This can happen even in the midst of a pious community.[2]

By reporting his behavior to the church leaders, Andy's friend gave him a jolt. "Like a cold shower of ice water," he added, letting out a deep belly laugh, lightening the mood. "But looking back, I can't say it wasn't the right thing to do. Pride had a hold on me. That time for me was really tough, really humiliating, but it was also cleansing. I don't think I could have kicked the habit of pornography alone. It's pretty insidious. And maybe my story can help someone else."

Andy has no doubt that his friend's motivation was in the right place. Their friendship was not only restored but made stronger. "There's a lot of trust in our friendship now. I know he's got my back, and he knows I've got his."

 ## REFLECTIONS ON PEACEMAKING

Confessing sin is a touchy subject. It's our nature to keep our failings utterly private. Public confession isn't common in our modern-day churches, but it is a part of many church traditions. Catholics practice private confession to a priest; Amish practice public confession. The early church of Acts found that it was strengthened, not weakened, by the confession of sins (Acts 19:17–20). What keeps you from confessing your faults to others? Pride? Shame?

How would you feel if a friend confided her flaws or failings to you? Chances are good that your friendship would grow even closer. Oddly enough, people are attracted to honesty and vulnerability. "You can't whitewash your sins and get by with it; you find mercy by admitting and leaving them" (Prov. 28:13 Message).

In *Life Together*, Dietrich Bonhoeffer wrote that "a man who confesses his sin in the presence of a brother knows that he is no longer alone with himself; he experiences the presence of God in the reality of the other person."[3] At first read, you might think that Andy's friend betrayed his confidence. Knowing the end of the story, do you think he did the right thing or the wrong thing?

Where do you seem to be stuck? What do you believe or feel you should do but just don't have the willpower to do it?

Based on the Bible's teachings, the Amish have a God-centered understanding of sin. While a sin often harms another, ultimately all sin is against God. "Against you, you only, have I sinned," King David wrote (Ps. 51:4 NIV). How does that belief affect your view of your own sins?

Confession is so much more than just admitting our short-comings. In an article called "When You Become the Thing You Hate," Max Lucado wrote, "[Confession is] radical reliance on the grace of God. A proclamation of our trust in God. His grace is greater than our sins. 'If we confess our sins, He will cleanse us.' There's certainty in those words. Not that He might, but that He will. Share all the details you can. Then let grace wash over you."[4]

 Plain *Truth*

"Like other people, the Amish forget, rebel, fall short, and for a variety of reasons, stray from their commitments. The rite of confession addresses deviance and restores backsliders to full fellowship. Minor transgressions are handled privately, but serious infractions require a public confession before the Gmay [church]. These can be cathartic moments when, the Amish believe, the power of the corporate church combines with divine presence to forgive and to purge the cancerous growth of sin."[5]

When Parents Make Mistakes

Joy from children is more precious than money.

Amish proverb

Last summer, Jeremy Chupp woke before dawn on a clear, cool, quiet Sunday morning. "We were going to have church at our place," Jeremy said. "That's always an exciting time for our children."

His ten-year-old son, Javin, had offered to get up extra early to help his father. "Dad, I'm gonna help you tomorrow," he had promised his dad.

Javin kept his word. "He was my little shadow that morning," Jeremy said. "First, we did the chores, then we took a walk to the neighborhood freezer building, approximately a quarter mile from our house. It was a picture-perfect morning, no one else was awake, all the houses were dark. It seemed Javin and I were the only people on earth. We talked softly the whole way as we walked. You could feel our hearts connect.

This was how God intended it to be between a father and a son."

Jeremy and Javin stopped at the shop building where church was to be held and lit the gas lights. "Because it was stuffy inside, I opened all the doors and windows and decided to set up fans to circulate some fresh air into the building. I found the fan I needed in the office area and plugged the twenty-five-foot extension cord into the inverter power strip where all the office equipment was plugged into. I handed the fan to Javin and told him to set the fan on the table outside."

There were two tables, one right outside the office by an open window and another across the room. Full of ambition and eagerness to help his dad, Javin took the fan and ran out the door toward the wrong table, the one that was over forty feet away. "The cord was only about half that long," Jeremy said, "but its length never occurred to Javin. Halfway across the shop, before I had time to blink, Javin reached the end of the cord and things began to happen inside the office. A small tornado! Cords, equipment, power strip and all moved along with him. And then, my nerves—already on edge because of the busy day ahead—vented. All at the same time. My human nature kicked in. I totally lost it. It wasn't pretty."

After the tornado of office stuff settled, Jeremy's angry words echoed into the light of daybreak. He saw his boy's heart break in two. "Right in front of my eyes. My words had cut that precious heart into shreds. Javin stayed with me, but not in my shadow anymore. He stayed away from me, dragging his feet and hanging his head. No more smiles, no more giggling. Silence, tension, and a crushed spirit. A dark cloud hung between us."

As the morning wore on, the two worked away, preparing for the church members to arrive. Javin did whatever Jeremy asked him to do, but then he'd sit down and hang his head.

"I knew I had some mending to do," Jeremy said. "But I was still focused on myself. I put it off in my mind. I'll talk to him this afternoon, I thought."

Another part of Jeremy, the more sensible part, said, *Do it now.*

I'll do it tonight when we're alone.

No. Not later. Now!

A battle kept waging within Jeremy. As father and son walked to the house to change clothes before the church people began to arrive, Jeremy stopped in his tracks. "I couldn't take another step. I turned and waited for Javin to catch up. He was dragging his feet behind me in the wet grass.

"I did have a reason to get upset. Everything I'd told him was the truth—but that was focusing on how I felt. The only way to his heart was to lay my feelings to the side and focus on how Javin felt."

With a lump in his throat, Jeremy turned to his son. "Javin, Dad really crushed your heart, didn't he?"

Tears welled up in Javin's eyes. Slowly, he nodded his head. "You made me feel terrible." His voice cracked as he spoke.

Jeremy put his hand on Javin's shoulder. "Javin, I'm sorry. I made a real bad mistake. I was wrong to talk to you like that. I know I hurt you inside and ruined your whole morning. I don't ever want to do that again. I love you, and you're special to me because you're my son. Your heart is precious to me, and I want to take care of your heart. I ask your forgiveness. From now on I just want to be here for you. Is that a deal?"

Javin looked up at his father. His face broke into a million-dollar grin. "Yep, Dad!"

Then something amazing happened. "As we walked up to the house, Javin started skipping and laughing again at my side. His heart was back in my hands already. Because I put away my feelings and focused on him, a heart was won again."

 ## Reflections on Peacemaking

Parents aren't perfect. All of us have parenting moments that are less than stellar, moments we're not proud of. When we acknowledge our shortcomings to our children, when we act quickly and seek to make amends, we're teaching them about humility. We're modeling how to restore a relationship.

In this particular situation, Jeremy was under pressure. The entire church was going to show up on his doorstep soon—that would make anyone feel stressed. But when he blew his top at his son, he had put church ahead of his son. To his credit, he took a moment to see the situation from his son's point of view. How does it help to understand the intention or thoughts of another?

Have you ever asked forgiveness from your child? What role does forgiveness play in the dynamic of your household?

Plain *Truth*

The Amish are the fastest-growing population in North America. "The population has doubled over the past 20 years due to sizeable families (5 or more children on average) and high retention rates (on average about 85 percent of Amish youth eventually join the church)." Because of these healthy growth and retention rates, "in most communities, over half of the population is under 18 years of age."[1]

Friendly Fire

Blunt remarks, like dull knives, often inflict the severest wounds.

Amish proverb

Catherine S. has a talent for turning a stranger into a friend in less time than it takes to say hello. And she values her friends—lifelong ones and those she just met in the grocery store line. She is a petite but vivacious woman, full of warmth, wisdom, and a clever way with words. She was raised in a very conservative Mennonite home in the Midwest, and describes herself as a compliant firstborn. "I was happy to be Plain," Catherine said. "I expected to be Plain my entire life. I never envisioned a day I would cut hair or wear a short dress. I never wanted to leave to do more 'stuff.'" Catherine married her high school sweetheart, Henry, and the couple had one son, then another, then two more. All boys! Even without a daughter, life was all she imagined it to be. More, even.

"But then came a time when we found ourselves in the middle of a storm of church controversy. It was over an issue we saw as very minor, something we had never hid from the ministry."

Henry, who worked as an accountant for a non-Mennonite business, was expected to wear a necktie with his suit coat. The financial community, across the country, still embraces the traditional suit and tie for men as daily garb.

To non-Plain ears, a tie is just a strip of silk. To the Plain community, a tie is a symbol of worldliness. "The ministry felt he would lose his identification as a Plain person," Catherine explained. "We never hid this from the ministry. My husband told them that he was only trying to support his family. But we were put under church discipline during communion and told not to receive communion because of that necktie."

In one fell swoop, Catherine, who had never caused an ounce of trouble in her life, was suddenly under church discipline. "This terrified me! We have to follow the rules!"

News traveled fast from one end of Catherine's small church to the other end. "I knew what a thriving grapevine it was. I knew how it worked. I used to talk about people who left. I remember how I felt and how I looked at those who had left. Gossip was sanctioned and rationalized—it was a way to hold people in tight. It was easier to criticize them and judge them. Small churches are so intertwined. We knew our ins and outs, everyone's weaknesses."

For the first time in her life, Catherine knew what it was like to be outside the circle of fierce protection. "I remember thinking that all of that Plain clothing was covering up strife and unrest. It was very deceptive because it had the appearance of righteousness." She's quick to add that not everyone in her church was gossiping about her and her husband. "Many demonstrated the love of Christ. It might have been easier for us to decide to leave if everyone was mean and nasty. But it wasn't that easy."

Henry ended up getting fired from his job. "For incompetence!" Catherine said. "There had never been anything but positive feedback for his work. Then," she snapped her fingers, "he suddenly gets fired." They had heard inklings that someone had called his boss about the necktie, and the boss, wanting to avoid a religious discrimination lawsuit, decided to let him go. "That stirred up the gossip even more. I felt so helpless. I couldn't even keep track of all of the rumors that were swirling around. I did know that the most hurtful ones came from those who were closest to us. It was as if they were trying to tell us, 'See what happens when you go against the church?'"

The heart of this issue was no longer about the importance of wearing clothing that identified a man with his Plain roots. The heart of this issue had become legalism. At its core, legalism is thinly veiled hypocrisy. A word with Greek roots, *hypocrisy* originally was used in the theater as a reference to an actor. It means "pretender" and had a neutral meaning until Jesus, who used the word twice to accuse the Pharisees and the scribes of feigning to be what they were not (Matt. 23:28; Luke 12:1). Ever since, the word has shifted to have a negative connotation.

Catherine said this experience made her take a hard look at her own habits. In particular, the habit of gossip. "Gossip is powerful. It always comes back to the heart. I had to think about what genuine love really looks like. You just don't run into gossip like you do in those small, legalistic churches. We didn't run into the gossip chains in the large church we began attending. Most of us didn't grow up together, and so you don't know everybody's business. Or history. Which makes it much harder for a gossip chain to thrive. I use 'chain' because it would literally thread its way from one Mennonite church to another one in other towns and communities close by. Unreal. There are those who can live in that environment and thrive, but I feel legalism has a view of a very demanding God. I look back now and think legalism becomes a spiritual stronghold of the Enemy. People aren't even aware how it kills the spirit."

After much prayer and soul searching, Catherine and her husband left their church over their growing dismay with its sanctioned legalism. "My own mother shunned me. It became a time when I discovered what Christ meant when He said that families will separate. I wasn't pleasing my family at the time, but I knew we were pleasing God. It wasn't easy, though."

Catherine, who cherishes and nourishes relationships, had to learn to be still and wait before God. One of her neighbors was particularly vicious. "She doesn't have a sharp tongue. She has a meat cleaver of a tongue. I had to learn to let the Lord vindicate me."

After they left their church, they discovered that daily life was more difficult without all the rules that ordained their lives. "I have to examine my motives and seek God's wisdom in all matters," she said. "I can't just follow rules."

In a phone interview about the topic of legalism, Ken Sande, president of Peacemaker Ministries, spoke about its inherent dangers. "The easy thing to do is to come up with absolutes," Sande said. "We don't have to think. But God calls us to think. It all goes down to the heart. That's how all must be filtered through."[1]

While Catherine's relationships with family and friends slipped into a strained distance, her relationship with God deepened. "That's how I coped with the pressure," she said. "I grew closer to the Lord.

"And I kept on being me. We live in the same area, even though we go to a different church. It's taken awhile. Sometimes, you just need to pull back for a while. There are some old friends who aren't going to be picnic buddies anymore. But I've forgiven them. I have peace."

And Catherine's husband ended up with a job offer for a company with higher pay and benefits than the company that laid him off. "When he received that job, I felt—but I didn't say—just look what happens when you put your trust in God."

 ## REFLECTIONS ON PEACEMAKING

There's an old Penn Dutch saying, "Criticism, unlike money, is easy to come by." We all have to learn how to deal with criticism, but it can have quite a sting when it comes from our church family, especially when we think we are doing what God asks us to do. When have you been a victim of friendly fire?

Catherine drew closer to God even as her church friendships felt strained. Doing this, she said, gave her peace. Can you describe a time when you handled criticism well? What about a time when you handled it poorly? What made the difference?

Developing a wall that deflects unconstructive criticism from a soft heart is just the right response. American Bible teacher Harry Ironside lived by this advice: "If what they are saying about you is true, mend your ways. If it isn't true, forget it, and go on and serve the Lord."[2]

 ## Plain *Truth*

"There are approximately 1,774,720 Anabaptists in the world, from Russia to Australia, California to China. They are farmers, government officials, businesspeople, stay-at-home parents, activists, missionaries, movie stars, bicycle mechanics, and auto workers. They speak Mandarin, Tshiluba, Spanish, English, Russian, French, and Pennsylvania Dutch. They are at the top rung of the economic ladder, and the bottom.

"So what is the connective tissue that holds this disparate global body together? Palmer Becker, a Mennonite pastor from Kitchener, Ontario, identifies three central elements.

- Jesus is the center of their faith.
- Community is the center of their lives.
- Reconciliation is the center of their work."[3]

It's Never about the Furniture

*Remember that the longer you carry a grudge,
the heavier it gets.*

Amish proverb

Early in their marriage, Fransene and Thomas had found a bargain on a beautiful wall unit at a thrift shop. "When we moved to our new homestead and tiny house," Fransene said, "I knew this was one set of furniture we may not be able to keep. Still, I hoped we could work something out. I'd always admired its beauty and had been hoping to keep it as an heirloom to pass on to our children." But when Fransene discovered that the wall unit was actually solid cherry, made by a very reputable company, and originally worth over $18,000, she felt more open-minded about selling it *if* they got a fair price for it. Otherwise, she would keep the parts they did have room for and sell the rest. "I was willing to sell if we got enough to make it feel worth the loss."

Unfortunately, there was a misprint on the ad, and the wall unit was listed for a bargain price. Fransene agreed to sell it to a buyer before she realized the price was listed incorrectly. "When I tried to tell her there was a mistake, she spoke rather unkindly and said I must keep my word." Fransene and Thomas were in a tight spot financially, outstanding bills hovering over their heads, and they agreed to the price listed in the ad. "But I felt completely forced into the deal," Fransene said. "It was a grievous way to see my much-loved furniture go."

She felt mad, powerless. "I know furniture has no eternal value and earthly possessions are only temporal, but the way this happened made me feel trapped and angry. It didn't help that my husband was happy about the sale because he could pay off a few bills that were weighing heavily on him. He didn't share my keen sense of loss or feeling robbed." So she stuffed her feelings down, down, down and became depressed.

This was a typical pattern for Fransene. She grew up in a church that emphasized forgiving and forgetting. "We were taught how we were supposed to respond. But I didn't know how to respond on the *inside*. I didn't know how to get healing from the inside. The pain inside, it has to be dealt with. There's a big need among our people about how to be honest on the inside. Honest about anger, frustration, how to resolve things."

The phrase "forgive and forget" misrepresents the true meaning of the work that goes into forgiveness. "The only way to truly forgive is by remembering," writes Gary Inrig in *The Risk of Forgiveness*. "We cannot make a simplistic connection between forgiving and forgetting. True forgiveness requires a careful look at what has actually happened. The central issue is not that we forget, but what we do when we remember that someone has wronged us."[1]

Also mistaken is the naïve assumption that "time heals all wounds." As Wheaton College psychology professor Dr. Mark McMinn says, "Time heals clean wounds. Soiled wounds fester and infect."[2] The same thing happens both in our inner being, Inrig writes, and in our relationships when we attempt to suppress the sins done to us. Denied offenses continue to pump poison into our life.[3]

After Thomas and Fransene had been married eleven years, they attended a Caring for the Heart seminar, led by John Regier, and were taught tools to reach into the past for unresolved issues and bring them to light for healing. They studied Scriptures that helped them get God's perspective on unresolved issues. "Now we have tools, so that when someone steps on our pain buttons, we know how to deal with it. We're not piling on more pain or building on old stuff."

But knowing what to do and applying it in the midst of a problem are two different things. Finally, everything about the furniture came to a head for Fransene. "I spilled my guts to Thomas and not in the nicest way." Things were tense for a little while. "It took both of us time and prayer to look past our own hurts and care about the other one."

As it turned out, Thomas had not fully realized how attached Fransene was to that furniture, and how helpless she felt about the sale of it. "When we let the sun set on our anger, we are giving ground to the Enemy. That's why I had depression and anger. God has to take back the ground. We have to ask Him to redeem the struggles.

"I'm so thankful for things the Lord has taught us about resolving conflict and caring about each other. And I'm also thankful for the hours and hours we spent cleaning up past bitterness and hurts we'd brought into our marriage unknowingly. As we methodically went back through many past failures and hurts, taking them to Jesus and letting Him heal and forgive, it seemed like we would never be done. But eventually we came to a sense of peace and freedom to love each other in depths we never had before.

"That doesn't mean it's all rosy now, but we are equipped with tools to resolve root issues when conflict arises. A side benefit is being able to lead our kiddos in prayer for healing from Jesus when they are struggling."

Fransene and Thomas are parents to six children, four of whom are adopted. "Adding half-grown children to our home brings even more issues than children born and raised under our roof." They make a point of showing their children how to resolve problems with people, starting from the inside. "As parents, we can provide examples. We can lead them in prayer. That's what we've learned to do with our children, so that they're not controlled by anger or putting Band-Aids on problems."

Soon, Fransene said, the wound of that furniture was no longer quite as raw. "We learned some good lessons. It bothered me that it was so hard for me, and I'm thinking the Lord maybe needed to remove something that was too important. At any rate, I will always remember that furniture fondly."

✦ REFLECTIONS ON PEACEMAKING

How do you respond when someone steps on your pain buttons? Do you flare up, snap back, or stuff it down and ignore it?

There's a danger, Gary Inrig writes, of "quick forgiveness—a hasty verbal declaration that keeps us from processing the violation."[4] Quick closure may actually prolong the process. The other extreme is the temptation to slow forgiveness, an ongoing "I don't feel ready yet," which can be a subtle way of inflicting punishment on the offender. How would you describe a healthy process that fits between these two extreme positions?

C. S. Lewis observed in his book *Letters to Malcolm, Chiefly on Prayer*, "To forgive for the moment is not difficult, but to go on forgiving, to forgive the same offense every time it recurs to the memory—that's the real tussle."[5] What memory creates a tussle for you?

Rather than dismiss or ignore uncomfortable issues, Fransene learned to open her heart to pain and accept the consequences, to honestly face it. She found peace by taking old and new emotional hurts to Jesus: "This is how it feels. Can You speak to it? Shed light on it? And what do I do with how it makes me feel?"

Think of a wound in your life that continues to fester. What happens when you lift it up to Christ and ask Him those very questions? You might not sense immediate answers, but you've invited God into the conversation. Keep talking to Him and watch for His redeeming work (Rom. 8:28).

The ability to forgive, Fransene believes, comes from God. "I don't have to do it by myself. He heals the pain and helps us release the person who hurt us."

Plain *Truth*

"Since 1999 a handful of communities have opened Amish-operated mental health treatment centers in Michigan, Ohio, and Pennsylvania. These provide services for men, women, and couples in a religious atmosphere. Participants engage in Bible study, group sessions, and physical work. Lay Amish counselors administer medications and arrange for visits to off-site therapists and psychiatrists. . . . The emergence of Amish-related and Amish-operated organizations from birth centers to homespun mental health treatment centers illustrates a structural negotiation with modernity—new organizational forms that reflect aspects of formal organizations with a distinctive Amish imprint."[6]

Make Your Stuff

———— ⌒ ————

If we do not cut the peace pattern right, we will have scraps.

Amish proverb

E very Amish boy dreamed of his sixteenth birthday," Joe Wittmer said. "You could date. You got your own horse and buggy. You could go to Sunday Sings." There were three ways of going to a Sunday Sing. "The goody-goodies would go inside and sing. The fence crowders would come in and go out. Then there were the rowdies, who stayed outside. They might have a little home brew too."[1]

Joe Wittmer, if there's any doubt, was a rowdie.

Wittmer grew up as the fourth of six children in an Old Order Amish family living in rural Indiana in the 1940s and '50s. Twice a year, prior to communion, church members were told to "make your stuff." "It means you need to clean up your accounts. If you have a conflict with someone else, it's time to fix that. If you owe anyone money, you need to settle up. My dad used to say it was time to deal with rotten apples. If you can't be at peace when you take communion, it's a big deal. You might be 'put' from the church. Excommunicated, that is."

As an unbaptized teenager, Wittmer wouldn't have been allowed to stay in church to hear the confessions. Only the church members remained. "But we did listen in through the windows. We wanted to hear those confessions. Sometimes, you'd hear a young man or a young woman confess to premarital sex. Then it would be announced that this couple would be married on Thursday."

Confession, Wittmer said, was a good thing. "It was a way of getting it off your mind. It's good for the soul. Grief over sins was a shared thing. It's something that is engrained into our culture." Afterward, he said, his parents never judged or evaluated a person. "You could judge the action, but not the person. We weren't taught to deny our feelings, but to never judge someone. That's God's business."

Communion—the breaking of bread—has been central to the worshiping life of Christians since the book of Acts. But what exactly is the meaning of communion? The word literally means sharing, fellowship, participation by all. It's supposed to bring everyone together as one body. The same Latin root, *com* (with, together) + *unus* (oneness, union), is used for the words *common*, *community*, and *communicate*. "Communion is a somber, sober time," Wittmer said. "Much more so than in modern churches." After "making their stuff" with God and with others, the bond of community among the Amish is renewed and reinvigorated for another six months of life together.

Wittmer never did partake in communion in the Amish church because he was never baptized. In the 1940s and '50s, in Indiana, it was common for Amish children to attend public school. "School was a necessary evil so I could play basketball." The love of basketball kept pulling him along. Much to the disappointment of his parents, he left home at sixteen to finish high school, then college, then graduate school, rarely returning home.

Wittmer always thought he'd return home one day, settle down, and join the church, as so many Amish teens do. There is a retention rate of 85 to 90 percent in the Amish church. But returning home permanently never quite happened for Joe Wittmer. "There was tenseness there. It was better not to be there. My family wouldn't want to eat with me. When I did visit, I would sit and eat first at the big table. Men would sit and talk with me, but they wouldn't eat. Then they would eat and I would sit and talk." He laughed. "I didn't mind so much, because I got to eat first."

It took about five or six years, Wittmer said, for things to get good again at home. "The transition to leave wasn't easy. Two cultures were always pulling at me. It took a toll, emotionally and psychologically."

The Amish would say "the world claimed him." But he disagrees. His life's work as a scholar has given him the opportunity to be a staunch defender of the Amish and their chosen way of life. He has a great respect and regard for his heritage. Wittmer eventually became the vice-chairman of the national Committee for Amish Religious Freedom, the organization that defended the Amish right not to attend high school all the way to the US Supreme Court in 1972 and won a unanimous decision.

Wittmer wouldn't change the path his life took, but did admit that there's always a void. "There's an authenticity in the Amish life. They really live what they learn, and they learn what they live."

Reflections on Peacemaking

Each time we gather to take communion, we are invited to become something bigger than ourselves: part of a community of faith, part of the body of Christ. Has receiving communion been only a private moment for you? Is it a communal moment? How might it be both?

Joe Wittmer said that his church was encouraged to "make their stuff" before taking communion. What would it mean to you, and to your church, if everyone took "making your stuff" seriously prior to communion?

What brings you to the communion table? What part of it affects you the most and why?

As you take leave of the Lord's table, how will it affect the rest of your week? Ideally, you go in peace to your home, your work, and your community (see John 6:51).

 ### Plain *Truth*

The Old German Baptist Brethren church, part of the post-Reformation Anabaptists, holds communion once a year and refers to it as a "Lovefeast." It's considered a holy occasion for the church—a time of seeking to strengthen the bonds and the spirit of harmony, goodwill, and congeniality, as well as to forgive past disputes. A time of community, a time of communion.

The Old German Baptist Brethren began as a small movement in Schwarzenau, Germany, during the early 1700s. They practice adult baptism by triple immersion or dunking—one for the Father, one for the Son, one for the Holy Spirit—and became known as the "Dunkers," which evolved into today's more common term of "Dunkards."

The Stories We Tell
Our Children

Purpose, not suffering, makes a martyr.

Amish proverb

Every American schoolchild has been told and retold two stories about American heroes. One is about George Washington, who cut down a cherry tree in his father's orchard (no one seems to know why) and then, when asked, didn't lie about it. The other is about Abraham Lincoln, who walked three miles to return a borrowed book. These stories not only remind children of their deep American roots, but also teach them lessons about how to manage life: Don't lie, don't cut down your father's fruit orchard without asking permission, follow through on promises, and value books.

Two similar stories are told and retold to every generation of Amish children; both are true, both beloved. These stories teach Amish children how to respond to those who treat them unfairly—whatever the cost.

The first comes from the *Martyrs' Mirror*, a book of early martyrs that can be found in most every Amish home. Dirk Willems was a sixteenth-century Dutch Anabaptist with a bounty on his head in those unhappy times. The 1500s was a period of intense persecution for the Anabaptists by authorities—if captured, they were executed. Dirk's crime was that he had been rebaptized in his late teens and he had allowed secret meetings to be held at his house in Asperen, Holland, meetings for preaching and for baptisms.

One late winter day, a thief catcher was hotly pursuing Dirk, followed by an official called the burgomaster. Dirk came to an expanse of water covered with the cracking ice of early spring. He hesitated a moment and then dashed across, followed by the thief catcher. Dirk made it across, but the thief catcher broke through the thin crust. Dirk made it to the far shore and could have easily escaped. No one in his church would ever criticize him for running on.

But in a dramatic expression of nonresistant love, Dirk turned back to rescue the thief catcher from the icy waters. The *Martyrs' Mirror* says he did it "quickly," probably with very little deliberation.[1] The thief catcher, after he had been pulled out of the water, wanted to let Dirk go. But the hard-hearted burgomaster, standing safely on the other shore, shouted that the thief catcher must arrest Dirk. He reminded him he had sworn an oath to fulfill his office, and if he broke his oath, he faced a fearful punishment. Reluctantly the thief catcher brought Dirk back.

Dirk was found guilty and was burned at the stake on a day so windy that his agony was prolonged.

Now fast forward two hundred years, across the Atlantic Ocean to the frontier of Pennsylvania. Amishman Jacob Hochstetler had emigrated from Rotterdam on the 1738 sailing of the *Charming Nancy*. He settled in the Northkill area (later known as Berks County) and lived with his family in relative peace until 1755, when tensions escalated on the Pennsylvania frontier from the French and Indian War.

Numerous Indian raids on settlers made the small Amish community, including the Hochstetler family, increasingly nervous. In the middle of a September night in 1757, a commotion was heard outside the Hochstetlers' door. One of Jacob's sons opened the door and was shot in the leg by an Indian. He reached for his rifle, but his father stopped him, insisting that it was against their principles to take human life. The house was set on fire by the Indians. As the family tried to escape through the cellar window, Jacob's wife, a son, and a daughter were caught and scalped. Jacob and his remaining two sons, Joseph and Christian, were taken captive and held for several years. As tensions eased between the Indians and the British government, they managed to return to Northkill.

Dirk Willems and Jacob Hochstetler are held up as examples—heroes, if you will, though they would have bristled at the word. By passing down such stories of martyrdom and persecution, each new generation is reminded that, to follow Christ's example, it's better to suffer and even die for the faith and to forgive their tormenters than to enter the cycle of violence that comes with trying to settle scores. To trust God to settle the scores, in His time.

In an ironic twist for a village that once sought to kill Dirk Willems, there is now a street in Asperen, Holland, named Dirk Willemszstraat.

REFLECTIONS ON PEACEMAKING

Dirk Willems and Jacob Hochstetler faced haunting choices. Both men acted out of their deep convictions not to repay evil for evil (see 1 Peter 3:9). If you were in either man's situation, what might have been your response to those "enemies"?

Not many of us will be faced with such haunting choices, but we do face a steady diet of smaller occasions to do good to those who hurt us. What would it look like for you to love an enemy?

When and what was the last time you repaid good for evil? How did it feel?

 ### Plain *Truth*

"Although the Anabaptist movement was never large, it accounted for 40 to 50 percent of all Western European Christians who were martyred for their faith during the sixteenth century."[2]

A Turned Cheek
and a Loaf of Bread

---

*The human heart, at whatever age, opens only to
the heart that opens in return.*

Amish proverb

Folks say there are three seasons in New England: winter, mud, and bugs. On a muggy and muddy spring day in upstate New York, five-year-old Mary Ann and her younger brother, John, followed their father out to the woods behind their farmhouse. Earlier in the morning, Mary Ann's father had dug holes for fence posts and pounded the posts into the ground. In the heat of midday, he was stringing wire along those fence posts. The topography in the area is scrubby, wooded, and hilly; rather than open pastures, the cows graze among the trees. Despite the languorous movement of cows, they have a tendency to roam and show up in someone's backyard, so fences are needed to keep them contained. Trotting behind her father, Mary Ann carried a little pail filled with horseshoe-shaped nails. Each time they came to a post, her father would hold out his hand to her and she would hand him a nail to hammer the wire in place. The wire was so taut that it zinged if John flicked it with his small fingers.

Suddenly, a burly man with formidable, upswept eyebrows appeared, a long shotgun gripped tightly in his hands. His face was sun-leathered and etched with deep lines; gray hair flopped over his forehead. He aimed his shotgun directly at Mary Ann's father and shouted at him to stop what he was doing, that he was trespassing on private property. Terrified, Mary Ann grabbed John's hand and pulled him to hide behind a tree. Cautiously, she dipped her head around the tree trunk to see what was happening.

Mary Ann's father stood stone still, hands on his hips, listening to the man rant and rave. Waiting a moment or two until the man's outrage wound down, her father finally spoke, in an even voice as calmly as if he were discussing the day's warm weather. "Well, then, where do you think the property line is?"

The man pointed out a marked trail—two feet away from the fence posts that Mary Ann's father had dug. "I don't want a fence so close to my land," the man sputtered. "I don't want your animals to reach through the fence and eat my grass. Not a blade of grass!"

Slowly, Mary Ann's father nodded. The man lifted his shotgun one more time, for emphasis, then spun on his heels and left, satisfied that he had gotten his message across.

So her father began to reverse the process of what he'd been doing all day—loosening all the nails that held the wire to the posts. Then he started pulling and tugging all the fence posts he had dug out of the ground. It was hard work, and her father looked tired and warm.

After the posts were pulled, her father re-dug the holes, several feet away from the marked trail. No cow, even if it stretched its neck as far as it could, would be able to reach even one tiny piece of grass through the fence.

When the fence was finally finished, they went back to the farmhouse, sweaty, hot, tired, hungry. As Mary Ann neared the house, she smelled a heavenly scent—she'd forgotten! It was baking day for her mother—and her stomach started to rumble. There was nothing she and John loved more than a thick slice of warm-from-the-oven bread, slathered in creamy yellow butter. Cooling on racks on the kitchen counter were loaves of golden brown, freshly baked bread. As Mary Ann's father told her mother about the angry man, he kept glancing at the cooling bread. "I'd like to take him a loaf of your baked bread."

After supper, Mary Ann's mother wrapped the loaf of bread in a tea towel, and her father drove away in the little open buggy. Mary Ann whispered a silent prayer that the man's shotgun was put away.

She stayed by the kitchen window, waiting and worrying about her father. She was worried, but even at the age of five, she wasn't surprised by her father's response to the man. Quietly deferring to another is the Amish way. To always repay evil with good is a habit deeply rooted in Amish life, instinctive to Mary Ann's parents. *Uffgevva* is a Penn Dutch word that means "giving up." Mary Ann remembers many instances in which her parents were always willing to go the extra mile, to turn the cheek, to live out Jesus's words from the Sermon on the Mount. To give up, *uffgevva*, their right for justification or revenge.

By the time the sun was setting over the farmhouse, Mary Ann heard the familiar clip-clop sound of a horse and buggy before she could even see it and knew her father was coming home. She let out a deep breath, relieved. After putting the horse in the barn, he came inside, sat down in his chair at the kitchen table, and pulled his children onto his lap, Mary Ann on one knee and John on the other. The man's name, he said, was Harold Young. He seemed especially cheerful after he saw the loaf of homemade bread. "He looked a little sheepish. I'm not even sure he had told his wife about the incident." Her father ended the conversation by adding, "Each time we think of Harold Young, we should try to think of something nice to say or do for him."

It might surprise you to learn that the Amish are sociable with the English. They are usually good neighbors who enjoy reciprocal friendships with non-Amish people. In particular, they appreciate it when the English are willing to transport them for errands or emergencies.

One year later, Mary Ann's family sold their New York farm to relocate to Somerset, Pennsylvania, where there were more Amish families. At the time, the community in New York was shrinking to the degree that church leaders couldn't even find a teacher to teach school. After the house was packed up and emptied out, the Youngs came to say their good-byes to Mary Ann's family. "Saying good-bye to Harold Young was particularly sad," Mary Ann said. "Years later, we returned to New York and made a point to go visit him. He was so pleased that we remembered him."[1]

All because of a turned cheek and a loaf of homemade bread.

❖ REFLECTIONS ON PEACEMAKING

In Amish life, silence has a purpose. Mary Ann's father listened to the neighbor's complaints, but he didn't object or interrupt. How did his response of silence keep the man's anger from escalating out of control? Why was that important?

Most everyone has a neighbor who creates problems— unreasonable or difficult or neglectful of property. Imagine facing a shotgun over your property line! A natural reaction, metaphorically, is to build a taller fence. Ignore the neighbor, look for small ways to get even. Yet look what happened when Mary Ann's father extended the olive branch. What might happen in your neighbor if you were to do the same?

To always repay evil with good is a habit that is deeply rooted in Amish life, as instinctive to Mary Ann's parents as it is incomprehensible to outsiders. Turning the other cheek means not returning insult for insult, which is what most people expect. Responding to hatred with love just might grab someone's attention and afford a chance to share the gospel. When we respond in a manner that is unnatural, it displays the supernatural power of the indwelling Holy Spirit.

Think back on your day today. Was there any opportunity to turn the other cheek, to give both cloak and coat, to go the extra mile?

Plain *Truth*

"Had the early Amish settlers not relocated in order to solve their problems, such as finding adequate and productive land, stability and unanimity in church discipline, and leaders who were committed to Amish principles, it is doubtful that they would have survived at all."[2]

Inside the Ring of Protection

*Forgiveness is the fragrance that the flower leaves
on the heel of the one who crushed it.*

Amish proverb

Joey B. was born with a burr under his saddle, said Ada, his mother. "Draw a line in the sand and he won't just cross over it, but jump over." Joey was Ada's ninth child, her last, and the most difficult one to raise. "It got harder when Joey reached his teen years," Ada said. "My husband died right about the time Joey turned thirteen, when he needed a father the most."

Joey was attracted to trouble, Ada said. "He ran around with a gang of rowdies, stayed up all night partying. He got into fights and caused some property damage." Only fifteen, Joey would arrive home at dawn and sleep till noon. Ada talked to him until she was blue in the face. "Joey would just say that he was only having a little bit of fun, that he was fine."

But things weren't fine. Joey's drinking and drug use started to spiral out of control. He had a few brushes with the law. Then came the lowest point. "Joey had been drinking for two days straight—binge drinking, it's called—and he plowed someone's car right into the phone shanty on our road and toppled it. Thankfully, no one was hurt—but it was humiliating. It even bothered Joey—because he couldn't avoid seeing it every day. I don't think it occurred to him that he was causing damage until he could actually see that knocked-down shanty."

The Amish don't have telephone service inside their homes, but it's customary for a group of Amish families living nearby to share a community phone in an unheated telephone shanty. The shanties look a little like an outhouse, tucked close to the road, and are used to give and receive telephone calls and messages.

Joey told Ada that he wanted to go live with his older brother in another community and she thought it sounded like a good idea. "We figured it might be best for Joey to have a fresh start. To get him away from that gang of rowdies, away from here, where he has a reputation of being a troublemaker. It's gotten so bad that whenever there's any problem in our area, everyone assumes it was Joey's doing."

To her surprise, the church leaders asked her to reconsider that decision. "I thought they'd be happy to see him go. But they told me that everyone had an interest in seeing Joey through these difficult years. A few even told me stories about their worst teenage mistakes."

A minister asked Joey to work for him in his carpentry shop. "Not asked," Ada corrected. "*Told* him to show up for work. Joey was angry at first. He doesn't like anyone telling him what to do. But this minister seems to know how to work with a boy like Joey. His wife said it's because he was a lot like Joey when he was young. It seems to be making a difference. As far as I know, Joey hasn't been out with the rowdies for a while."

Ada is cautiously hopeful that Joey is growing up. "Maybe that knocked-down phone shanty was God's wake-up call." Her eyes lifted upward, hopefully, at that last sentence, as if sending up a prayer.

In ancient times, people who did damage to a town were sent to live outside its walls, beyond the pale, or boundary, beyond community, beyond inclusion and protection. This Amish church wanted Joey inside the pale, inside the ring of protection.

A similar community response, though non-Amish, happened in California in 1995, at the Point Reyes National Seashore. Four teenage boys camped illegally overnight at Mount Vision, built a campfire, and in the morning took great care to extinguish the fire. Then they left.

For two days, the fire continued to smolder under the pile of dirt and rocks. Winds started to pick up and fan the embers, triggering a wildfire that consumed 12,000 acres of wilderness area, burned forty-five homes, and cost $6.2 million to suppress. Helicopters saved the town of Point Reyes with water from the bay; the water was dropped on the pine forest between the town and the burning ridge. But the loss of wildlife was unimaginable: birds, deer, coyote, bobcats, mountain lions, beavers. It was described as if a bomb had fallen.

The four teenage boys who had accidentally started the fire turned themselves in to the police as soon as they realized what they'd done. Their parents stood beside them. The boys had no idea they had left behind a smoldering disaster in the makings. One of the boys' handprints was found on top of the pile they had made—proof that they had checked for radiant heat. They were not prosecuted but ended up doing community service.

The president of the board of firefighters heard that the families were considering leaving the area. In a speech given to honor the firemen who fought so bravely to put out the Mount Vision fire, he said the town should make clear to the families that they wanted the boys to stay. His speech received sustained applause. People whose houses had burned down came up to the speaker to tell him they agreed with him. They wanted the boys inside the pale, inside the ring of protection.

And so the families didn't move.[1]

 ## REFLECTIONS ON PEACEMAKING

Community is a complicated word. It means different things to different people. It's an emotive concept that can trigger feelings of security, awaken a longing, or perhaps just create mild curiosity. How would you define community? And why is community important?

These two stories are examples of forgiving communities. One person in each, though, initiated the process and spearheaded the journey to forgiveness. Who might that leader be in your community (family, church, neighborhood)?

What difference do you think it made to Joey, and to those four teenage boys, to be asked to remain "inside the ring of protection"?

A public library in Buchanan County, Iowa, doubles as the community center. Many latch-key children spend weekday afternoons in the library. So many that the librarians decided to provide homework help and tutoring. They *know* these children. If anyone acts up or causes a problem, one librarian said, he has to write his name on a list and not return for a day. What benefits occur when a community takes action and cares for its young people—in other words, when they keep them inside the ring of protection?

 Plain *Truth*

"The Amish stress the importance of adult baptism. In their late teens and early 20s, Amish youth decide if they want to join the church. If they choose to be baptized, they submit themselves to the order of the church for the rest of their lives. Candidates make a confession of Christian faith and agree to comply with the order and discipline of the community, known as the Ordnung. The unwritten Ordnung shapes Amish life and identity. Passed on by oral tradition, it spells out expected behaviors—wearing Amish clothing, using a horse and buggy, placing steel wheels on farm machinery, and using gas appliances. The regulations also forbid certain behaviors—divorce, going to college, attending theaters, filing law suits, owning cars, and using self-propelled farm equipment."[2]

PART TWO

TURNING
POINTS

———— ⌒ ————

Forgiveness is better than revenge, and in the long
run a lot cheaper.

Amish proverb

I n 2006, Australian wildlife expert Steve Irwin—known as the Crocodile Hunter—was filming an underwater documentary at the Great Barrier Reef when a stingray barb pierced his chest, fatally wounding him. In the weeks after Irwin's death, mutilated stingrays were found washed up on the beaches of Queensland, Australia. What motivated such misguided carnage by Irwin's fans? Revenge.

The desire for revenge is the most powerful cause of violence that social psychologists have identified. About one in five violent assaults and murders are motivated by vengeance. Today, terrorist organizations recruit human bombs by taking advantage of that desire for revenge.

Some say that you could write the whole history of the world in terms of the history of revenge. The desire for revenge after being mistreated has been identified in virtually every human society. Anthropologists found that the need to "get even" was probably one of the earliest motives for war and drove much of the destruction seen over the centuries.

Throughout history, we've had an insatiable fascination with stories of vengeance. From the earliest Greek tragedies, to the Bible, to Shakespeare, retribution fuels the stories that people find important, memorable, and entertaining. In old Greek and Roman ruins, all over the ancient Mediterranean world, archaeologists have discovered stored prayers known as curse tablets. They were a means of revenge. Some of the earliest examples, dating to the fifth century BC, have been discovered in the Greek colonies on Sicily, and the practice extended to Roman Britain, where over one hundred curse tablets from the second and third centuries AD have been recovered from the natural hot springs at Bath, England. The curses generally followed a simple formula: invoke the name of the gods, describe the desired punishment, name the victim, and explain why they have incurred your wrath. A number of the tablets from Bath, England, spewed curses on thieves who stole clothing while the innocent victim was enjoying the healing waters!

How many "bless my enemy" tablets do you think archaeologists have found? None. Not *one*.

There's a rise of revenge in popular culture, such as the hit television show *Revenge*. There are websites dedicated to revenge, such as getrevengeonyourex.com, where jilted lovers can hire help and share stories to get even with their former partners. "Legally and effectively," the website states playfully. The business is thriving.

Revenge even *feels* good. Scientists have found that the dorsal striatum, the part of the brain that sends reward signals, is stimulated when people desire revenge. It triggers an adrenaline rush. It's powerful, it's addictive. Wilma Derksen, mother of a murdered child, said that a friend asked her what it would take to feel satisfied that justice had been served. Wilma said she wanted to line ten child murderers up against a wall and shoot them. "And I wanted to be the one to pull the trigger," she said. "And it felt *delicious*." She laughed at herself. "So much for my Mennonite peace-loving background."[1] (See Wilma's story in the next chapter, "The Unthinkable.")

Revenge is a natural response to being wronged. (If you don't think this is true, just picture yourself driving in stressful traffic situations and see if anything comes to mind.) You could even say revenge is an intuitive desire for justice, for fairness, for the protection of rights. The difference between revenge and justice is a very subtle one. Acting on feelings of revenge can be dangerous and ultimately self-destructive. Obsessive, even.

In the upside-down world of Christianity, the Bible brings a very different kind of message: to bless and pray for our enemies, to leave revenge in God's hands, to trust in His perfect justice, relieving us of the burden of repayment. "Don't insist on getting even. That's not for you to do. 'I'll do the judging,' says God, 'I'll take care of it'" (Rom. 12:19 Message).

The Amish rely on a trust in divine providence to make sense of events that seem senseless. Choosing to forgive doesn't mean they condone bad behavior or erase its consequences. But it does mean they are satisfied to leave legal ramifications in the hands of the law and thereby avoid that slippery path into vengeance. Their entire world perspective rests on the sovereignty of God. They can leave justice in God's hands because they have a quiet confidence that in the end God will be a merciful and just judge. They believe God will, indeed, ultimately "take care of it."

Maybe one of the reasons the Amish are better prepared to forgive others is that they don't expect life to be fair. The habit of forgiveness is so deeply ingrained in how the Amish view the world—so much a part of who they are—that when things do go wrong, they're already in a forgiving mode, so the problem doesn't have a chance of growing into a story of resentment.

Life isn't fair.

Sounds so simple it's almost laughable. But recognizing that truth creates a shift in our worldview. If we accept that life isn't fair, when bad things do occur, they don't turn our world upside down. They don't overwhelm and derail us. And before they ever take place, we have a tool to deal with them.

Forgiveness is the tool that enables you to handle life rather than be overwhelmed by it, writes Dr. Dick Tibbits in *Forgive to Live: How Forgiveness Can Save Your Life*. He suggests you keep in mind the following two principles:

1. The more important forgiveness is to you, the more likely you are to forgive.
2. The more often you practice forgiveness, the more forgiving you become.[2]

Making forgiveness a habitual way of thinking completely changes your experience of life. It doesn't take away the hurt, the disruption, or the undesirability of the offense, but it gives you the ability to deal with the offense rather than be overwhelmed by it. With this orientation toward forgiveness, you refuse to expend a whole lot of energy thinking about how others have wronged you. Instead you use your energy to focus on what you need to do to achieve your most important life goals.

Most of the following stories contain events that I pray we never have to face in our lives. Still, there are many things we can learn from them—lessons of forgiveness to teach us about letting go and moving on. Today's daily choices do indeed have long-term consequences—for our immediate health and well-being, and possibly for our eternal destiny.

John Piper, in his sermon called "Forgive Us Our Debtors," sums it up in a way that is difficult to dismiss:

> The greatest risk we face as a church in these days is not that we may lose an organ, or that we may lose money, or that we may lose members, or that we may lose staff, or that we may lose reputation. The greatest risk is that we may lose heaven. Because one way to lose heaven is to hold fast to an unforgiving spirit and so prove that we have never been indwelt by the Spirit of Christ. If we hold fast to an unforgiving spirit, we will not be forgiven by God. If we continue on in that way, then we will not go to heaven, because heaven is the dwelling place of forgiven people.[3]

The ultimate goal of living the forgiving life is to move from forgiveness as a tactic for *coping* with a specific conflict to forgiveness as a strategy for *living*. For today and for all your tomorrows.

The Unthinkable

Revenge appears to be love, as a wrong dressed up in right.

Amish proverb

On an ordinary Friday afternoon in November 1985, Wilma Derksen was cleaning up the basement when her thirteen-year-old daughter, Candace, called and asked for a ride home from school. Busy with two other children, trying to finish the task she had started, Wilma asked Candace if she had bus fare (she did) and to please just come home on the bus.

Candace didn't come home. They called her friends, searched the streets, went to the police, and yet nobody could find her.

Almost near dawn after Candace's disappearance, Wilma noticed that the wind had stopped. "I hadn't even realized there had been a wind, or even the sound of wind. Now in its absence, the silence, the stillness, was deafening and hor-rific. The struggle had stopped."[1] She sensed what it meant.

Somehow, Wilma wrote, the heavens were still open, and Candace's presence seemed to fill the room. Candace was close, but yet so far—just out of reach. "I wanted to enter fully into the next dimension, to ask her if she was okay, to ask her who had taken her away, but a soft, black velvet curtain fell between us and shut me out. She was gone."[2]

It was just a feeling Wilma had, not based on any evidence. She shared this experience only with her husband, Cliff, be-cause she didn't want the police to slow down or cease looking for Candace. After all, it was just a feeling.

For seven long weeks, despite massive police and civilian searches scouring the city of Winnipeg, no one knew where Candace was or what had happened to her. It wasn't until January when the police found her frozen body, hands and feet tied, in a shed not far from their home. She had died that first night, just as Wilma had sensed.

On the evening of the discovery of Candace's body, a man knocked on the Derksens' door and said he had a message for them. Wilma vaguely recognized him and invited him inside. He introduced himself as the father of a murdered child. He came, he said, to tell them what to expect, what lay ahead for them. For the next two hours, he described every detail of his daughter's murder, the police case, the trial. By the time he left, the Derksens were thoroughly exhausted. Terrified too.

The man's life was a picture of someone obsessed with revenge. "Revenge is seductive," Wilma said. "It's energy. It makes us feel good. It's . . . delicious. It's addictive. And there's a lot of rationale for righteous anger."[3]

But the toll of revenge, Wilma saw in this visitor, was profound. The murder of this man's daughter had destroyed his life, his marriage, his health, his ability to work. So much loss.

It dawned on Wilma and Cliff that their faith in God gave them another option, another resource. "I was so young when this hit me," Wilma said, "such a young woman. But as young as I was, I had a base. I had an alternative to vengeance: forgiveness."

They came to the conclusion that in order to be free to live again, they would need to forgive the individual who had killed their daughter.

"I'm so glad we made that choice. It didn't spare us everything, but it did spare us much. Our marriage is still intact. Our other two children are doing well.

"Forgiveness was letting go of the need for vengeance. It was our way to stop focusing on the evil done to us." It took time, she said. "Forgiveness takes patience. Justice takes time. God is on the side of the victim."

But revenge, she said, is the Evil One's path. "The Evil One's path is destructive—it doesn't lead to good. God has given us controls over our choices. If we give our victimization to God and don't become offenders ourselves, then we won't cut off our mercies. God works tiny little miracles in our lives, but the minute we hurt or damage another, we cut ourselves off from His mercies. We cut God off. He can't give to someone who doesn't love. He can't empower us to do evil. We go into Enemy territory. There is no mercy there. We're on our own and that's a scary place to be. I can feel it! The empowerment of God is not there. I'm allowed to make that choice. But when I choose to give my victimization to God, His love is multiplied."

One of the most difficult things Wilma faced was to forgive herself for not picking Candace up on that November afternoon.

On the anniversary of Candace's disappearance, almost to the minute, Wilma noticed Candace's fingerprints still on the stair wall. Suddenly, she wrote in her memoir, accusations came flying. "Why hadn't I picked her up? What kind of mother would allow her daughter to walk home in the cold at such a vulnerable time? Why hadn't I foreseen what was going to happen? Why hadn't we been able to convince the police to get out the dogs when the scent was fresh? We had done nothing! While she froze to death in a shed, we had been sitting in a warm house just waiting for her to die.

"It was all my fault," she continued. "I could have prevented all of it from happening. Candace had died, and I had the audacity to survive and go on living." Wilma had avoided or suppressed those accusations for a year. "I tried to turn them off, but I had ignored them for a whole year, and it had only allowed them to grow stronger and uglier." She knew the hideous voices were totally irrational, but guilt is irrational. No matter how hard she tried to reason with it, she still felt guilty. "I needed to deal with this feeling on a feeling level." She needed to allow herself to feel what she'd ignored so the guilt could be dealt with.

When Candace had encountered problems in school, such as being seated next to a bully, Wilma had always emphasized a loving response. It was the Mennonite way—to turn the other cheek, to repay good for evil. "I would tell her that love was the most powerful weapon there was." Now, she wondered, had Candace met an oversized bully and tried to use the weapon of love?

"That was tough. I had failed. We want to be that perfect mom. Not being able to protect your child—oh, it's hard to allow yourself to be human. We do fail our children. We do let them down. Moms feel this in millions of ways."

Wilma looked back over the year and realized, quite understandably, that she had been filled with anger and rage. At first, it was anger directed toward the murderer. But now she had started to forgive the person, though still unidentified, who had actually committed the crime. Next, she faced the anger she felt toward the police for being ineffective. In retrospect, she realized that her expectations for the police were unrealistic, and that lessened the blame she felt toward them.

But that left a large amount of guilt and rage still to cope with and no one to blame. No one but herself. If she was able to forgive the person who had actually done the crime, why couldn't she forgive herself? But where could this guilt go? "Who could bear this guilt and rage? Who could really deal with it?"

And suddenly Wilma saw the cross. "Better than ever before, I understood why Christ had to die. I finally knew where I needed to go with all the guilt."

Wilma had always thought forgiveness was a means to bridge broken relationships with others. "In some weird way," she wrote, "the whole concept of forgiveness wasn't for everyone else, it was for me. It was a way to acknowledge others' fallibility and give them room to fail. I had never really thought that this same forgiveness would, in some way, be there to heal the broken relationship within me as well. It was the glue that would keep me together and save me from falling into a million different pieces."[4]

Forgiveness, Wilma believes, is needed every day. "There are issues every day. There are choices every day. Do I show love? Or less love? Or no love?"

Wilma said that her Mennonite heritage taught her a combination of working out her faith by moving "into" love. As her journey continued, she became an activist. "I took on the responsibility of mothering Candace's memory." She became the founding member of Child Find Manitoba and is on the executive board of Victim's Voice. Currently, she's working on a Candace House Initiative, a building for victims of crimes.

Twenty-two years after Candace's body was found, the murderer was caught, convicted, and sentenced to first-degree murder. The long trial churned up all the feelings and uncertainty that the Derksens had dealt with, but as the trial concluded, Wilma and Cliff were satisfied that justice had been served.

And then, in 2012, the conviction was overturned. At the time of this interview, the Supreme Court of Ottawa, Canada, was scheduled to hear the case. Wilma said it's almost odd to see how large a role Candace continues to play in their lives. "Candace is still an entity. She is still a strong presence in our life."

Wilma is prepared to face the new trial and its outcome. "Back then, it was dark," she said. "I weather my storms better now than I did then. I used to head for the hills when facing controversy. But I'm not afraid. I'm not fearful. When we face a storm, we have to be in the front of the boat, facing the waves, letting the rain pour over us."

Imagine people weathering life's storms without any foundation, any base, like Wilma and Cliff had with their Mennonite beliefs. "But it doesn't have to be that way," she said. "All of our lives can be about setting up a good foundation."

REFLECTIONS ON PEACEMAKING

The night of Candace's disappearance caused Wilma to face an important question: Could she entrust her daughter's life to God? "I suddenly realized what the story of Abraham and Isaac was all about. Our children are not ours to keep. We are to give them back to God for His purposes, purposes that we don't always understand." How can having faith in the sovereignty of God give you confidence as you parent?

Life is always a test, Wilma said. The minute we think we have grasped some truth, life will test it for us. Often it comes in the form of the smallest choices. What choice did you face today that tested your beliefs?

On the first night of Candace's disappearance, Wilma had what she called an "experience." She knew her daughter was in heaven, she knew she was safe. Wilma said she wouldn't build a theology around that moment, but to her, it was very real. And very comforting. What kind of peace does Wilma's experience bring you?

 Plain *Truth*

In the last thirty years since her daughter's murder, Wilma Derksen has helped found numerous programs, including Child Find Manitoba, Family Survivors of Homicide, Safe Justice Encounters, Voice of Resilience, Victim Companions, and the Paying Forward Project. She has been invited to speak around the world on topics such as restorative justice, victims' rights, and forgiveness. She also serves as a trauma therapist. For more information about Wilma, go to www.wilmaderksen.com.

Twist of Faith

The lost need to be saved. The saved need to be healed.

Amish proverb

Nowadays, you can't walk through a mall or an airport without passing by an Auntie Anne's Soft Pretzel stand. The sweet scent of the baking pretzels is instantly recognizable, as if trademarked. But you might not be aware that the founders, Anne and Jonas Beiler, were once Amish. Jonas was raised in an Old Order Amish home, one of four children, had an eighth-grade education, and spent a great deal of time in the kitchen because his mother was bedridden. He also tinkered with everything and was always fixing broken objects. Anne was raised Amish-Mennonite. They had a storybook romance, Anne said, and married at a young age.

The Beilers have had a roller-coaster experience of a life—high highs with the phenomenal success of their family business, Auntie Anne's Soft Pretzels, and low lows with truly profound sadnesses.

Early in their married life, Anne and Jonas were faced with the accidental death of their two-year-old daughter, Angie. In her fresh grief, Anne sought out counseling with their pastor.

They were doing all the right things to recover from their grief, but something went terribly wrong. In the pastor's role as counselor to Anne, he took advantage of her—something called spiritual abuse of power. Afterward, he threatened her by saying that no one would ever believe her if she told what had happened between them. Defeated, broken, she accepted his manipulative words and his abuse.

Six *years* of abuse.

Anne started having serious stress-related health problems; her weight plummeted to ninety-two pounds. "I thought I was having a heart attack," Anne said.[1] In her distress, everything spilled out to Jonas.

"My best friend, my pastor, betrayed my family," Jonas said, his voice breaking over the words. "Simple Sunday school teachings don't work. 'Forgive and forget' does not work. 'Fake it till you make it' does not work. There are things that come along that make us rethink everything."[2]

But offering forgiveness to his wife wasn't even a question for Jonas. In his Old Order Amish home, he had been raised to move toward reconciliation. He loved his wife and daughters; he didn't want to have his marriage end.

"I hurt Jonas," Anne said, "but by his actions, he gave me forgiveness that day."

Jonas left behind his trade as an auto mechanic and became a counselor. He had a dream to provide a nonprofit counseling center to their community. Anne bought a small market stand to try to help support the counseling center—that's where the famous Auntie Anne's soft pretzel got its start.

So life began again for the Beilers.

The pretzel business was expanding at a breakneck pace, the counseling center was growing. But at home, even in the midst of enormous financial blessings, the Beilers' hopes and dreams for a stable family were crumbling.

Jonas and Anne found out that their youngest daughter had also been taken advantage of by that same man—their pastor. For over a year, Jonas suppressed his rage toward this man—but he also kept a knife with him. His year of revenge, he called it. He never acted on an impulse to kill the pastor, but he wanted to. "Maybe my year of revenge gave me the energy to get through the year. Revenge is empowering."

Here is how Jonas described the battle going on in his soul.

"God's still small voice broke through my rage. 'Do you really want to do this, Jonas?' In a teary voice, I would argue back, 'Yes, I really do.'"

God won that battle and Jonas relinquished his need for revenge. "Revenge," he says, "hidden deep in your spirit, causes undesirable consequences."

In his counseling practice, Jonas had observed a pattern in his clients. "In counseling, we need to open this [painful experience] up. To let it out. First, there's relief. Then they call and say they're depressed or exhausted. I call it 'the emotional hangover of opening up the lid.'" Jonas pointed out that many Catholics experience better emotional and physical health than mainstream society. "There's a study from the early 1970s that supports that. The Catholics have confession and forgiveness. The Amish are similar—when someone falls or fails, they're brought up to church to confess, to move on. My brother used to have boils that started with a pimple. My mom would say, 'It's not going to get better until the core comes out.' That's the way it is with people too. But we tend to put a lid on things."

He saw the same pattern in himself. He realized he had to stop bottling his feelings, had to learn how to process through them. "Suppressed feelings cause abscesses of the soul. I had to scream it out. David, in the Psalms, certainly felt anger and revenge. God is okay with whatever you feel." He has a saying: "If you're going to heal it, you've got to feel it."

Meanwhile, during that painful year, Anne struggled with her own feelings of shame and guilt over the pastor's abuse of their daughter. "Every time I came home, I felt pain. I was sinking into an abyss, going further and further and further. The Enemy reminded me of my failings."

In her despair and depression, she had a short-lived affair with a man she had recently met. "I realized that there was something very wrong at the core of me. I couldn't blame anyone for this."

Anne and Jonas received counseling to try to heal their marriage. The counselor told her, "Three strikes and you're out."

But Jonas told her something else. "I'm not quitting. I've put too much time, too much forgiveness into this marriage to quit." He repeated, "I'm not quitting."

Anne realized she had never truly believed she was forgiven—for betraying her husband, for not protecting her daughter, for sinning against God. "Grace was for anybody, but there wasn't enough left for me. My guilt and shame were abundant . . . even in the midst of great financial blessing."

One day, she experienced a "presence" in the room. "Jesus said—not audibly—'This is the Good News of the gospel. I have forgiven you. There is nothing more you can do. I died for your sins, all of them. And I did it for you. I'm sitting at the right hand of God, praying for you.'"

A response rose from deep inside her. "Yes, yes, yes! And I have never put on the cloak of guilt or shame again since that day. Like ocean waves, forgiveness keeps washing over me."

Jonas said that in the process of forgiveness he had to ask himself, Does my theology work? "It could be that it's time to take in new information, to help get unstuck. We have to settle our view of God. If our view of God isn't sound . . . we have to have it out with him. To depend on God's goodness, sovereignty."

Jonas and Anne (still married!) take many of the principles of reconciliation into their business model. If they have a conflict with a franchise owner, they go to the venue, sit down at a table, and work through the misunderstandings or miscommunications. They move *toward* reconciliation.

"Forgiveness is an everyday thing," Anne said. "We need it every single day." She says it's about redemption. "How do we glorify God in our life? The best way is by telling our story. It's all redemption."

 ## REFLECTIONS ON PEACEMAKING

Is there an area of your life in which you're stuck? Could it be, like Anne, that you struggle with forgiving yourself? How did Anne's experience of a "presence" speak to you?

In *Think No Evil*, Jonas wrote, "While there are many ways that we can be wronged, there are only two very distinct choices we can make after we are wronged: to forgive or to accuse."[3] By choosing to forgive his wife, he saved his family. Do you believe that a marriage can become good again? Why or why not?

"Forgiveness is a choice," Jonas says. "Everything else is a process." What are your thoughts about his comment?

Jonas has a high regard for his Amish upbringing. "What I liked about my childhood is that I learned God is with me all the time. If I have a good day, He is there. If I have a bad day, God is there."

 ## Plain *Truth*

In his book, *Think No Evil*, Jonas says that the Amish are far ahead of the rest of us when it comes to the concept of forgiving. "They forgive because they believe God's way is the best way to live. They know that when God commands us to do something like forgive someone 'seventy times seven,' it is not a capricious rule for us to follow, but part of a properly ordered life that is intended for our good. They don't pass these lessons on to their children just for the sake of tradition, but because they want their children to be free of bitterness and anger, too. That's why it's woven deep into their culture. They model this forgiveness for their children, along with their entire belief system, by living it out, and they are able to do it so well that the next generation does not wonder how things like this should be handled."[4]

Stuck in Bed

If we feel the storm, we know the worth of the anchor.

Amish proverb

---

ading light falls in rectangles from the windowpanes onto the worn brown couch where Linda F. is sitting. A black Labrador retriever with a white muzzle lies by her feet, thumping his tail now and then, without warning or reason. Linda is a soft-spoken, middle-aged woman who chooses her words slowly and carefully. She never married. She lives with her parents in a modest Amish farmhouse near Shipshewana, Indiana—the home where she was born. And the home where she spent two years convinced she was dying.

Linda's doctors couldn't agree on what was wrong with her—no test was conclusive. One doctor diagnosed her with fibromyalgia, another with Lyme disease, another with Epstein-Barr. She tried pills, nutritional supplements, reflexology, acupuncture. Nothing worked. Her body ached, her head ached, she felt constantly fatigued, she grew discouraged and depressed. She had to stop working as a waitress at a local restaurant for tourists—a job she enjoyed. She could barely stay on her feet through the course of a day. Finally, she just stayed in bed, waiting to get better. Or not.

One afternoon, a friend came to visit with a specific mission: she wondered if there might be an emotional cause to the illness, some reason as to why Linda was so sick and wasn't improving. She asked Linda if there was anyone in her life whom she hadn't forgiven. Or anyone whom she should ask forgiveness.

"I was stunned," Linda said. "Absolutely stunned. I didn't like hearing that. I had always tried to forgive and forget. But my friend said I might not really understand what forgiveness is. She said it's about finding peace."

After her friend left, Linda pondered her words. She knew that peace often eluded her. Bottled anger was always below the surface, kept in check but a constant companion. She could actually feel her face grow warm and her blood pressure rise, lying in bed, as she reviewed wounds she'd experienced. She reached for a pad of paper and a pencil. "Would you believe that I filled the page? It was shocking—so many grudges I had held on to. Some things were small, some big, but many things I remembered with a sting. I thought I'd forgiven and forgotten. I hadn't."

Her mind traveled to those whom she had hurt, guilt-ridden memories. Sharp words, careless remarks, selfish acts. She filled another page.

Linda decided that if she were going to die, she should leave this earth with her life cleaned up. Over the next month, she wrote a letter to everyone she had hurt over the years and asked for their forgiveness—twenty-seven letters in all.

And to the names on the list of those she realized she hadn't forgiven, one by one, she opened her palm, said a prayer, and offered forgiveness. She released each grievance, one by one. Even the hardest one of all—her anger at her estranged brother for things he had done.

It wasn't long until responses came back to Linda. "Not everyone answered back, but many people wrote and said they were very touched by my letter. A few were so moved by it that they did the same thing—they made a list of people they had hurt and sent them letters to ask forgiveness."

Waiting for the mail became the bright spot in Linda's day. Some wrote to tell her of their own struggles with buried hurts. "It's become my ministry," she said. "A letter ministry." She said she felt her life had some purpose, even as she was confined to bed.

About three months after her friend's visit, Linda's health started to improve—enough so that she could get out of bed for half the day, then most of the day. Two years later, her health is nearly fully restored.

Research is confirming what you might suspect: forgiveness is good for health, while holding on to hurts and grudges damages it. A study called the Stanford Forgiveness Project found startling results in participants who received six sessions of ninety-minute forgiveness training. They were significantly less angry than those who did not receive intervention. The participants in the forgiveness group also reduced stress symptoms such as headaches, stomachaches, dizziness, fatigue, and muscle aches. The implications for long-term health were equally significant—all the way to benefiting immune, hormone, and cardiovascular systems.[1] "A heart at peace gives life to the body," King Solomon wrote over four thousand years ago (Prov. 14:30).

And very possibly, helps one to live a long life.

In another study, Luther College psychologist Loren Toussaint and colleagues investigated the relationships among forgiveness, religiousness, spirituality, health, and mortality. They found that people who practice forgiveness may receive health benefits in multiple life-sustaining ways, including extending their life. People who forgive more readily are less likely to be depressed and anxious, and more likely to be happy. These physical and psychological qualities could all be key in predicting a longer life.[2]

Other studies have found that practicing forgiveness can reverse warning bells of ill health, such as high blood pressure. "Unresolved anger can lead directly to heart disease and other serious illnesses," wrote Dr. Dick Tibbits in his book *Forgive to Live*, "but by practicing forgiveness you can reverse harmful effects. In short, forgiveness is the work you need to do for your own health and well-being."[3]

Doctors still don't know what was wrong with Linda, nor do they know what cured her. Linda knows. "It was a sickness of my spirit. I was flooded with the wrong kinds of emotions." She became instantly animated, lifting her hands high. "But no longer."

REFLECTIONS ON PEACEMAKING

Did learning to forgive heal Linda F.? Maybe. It certainly facilitated her healing and helped her to cope with her circumstances. But the important thing to remember about Linda F.'s story is that buried hurts don't stay buried. Sooner or later, they have to be dealt with. In your own life, could there be a link between illness, healing, and reconciled emotions?

Blogger Bryan Bell attended a conference that challenged each person to seek reconciliation with those whom they have hurt. Convicted by the challenge, Bell made a list. He went to each individual, some of whom he had to track down, to apologize and ask for forgiveness. Afterward, he said it was the most beneficial thing he had ever done in his life. Not only was he freed of guilt, but broken relationships were restored and made whole.[4] Think for a minute of those whom you have hurt or offended. Have you ever asked those people to forgive you?

What would it take for you to seek out those whom you have wronged and initiate reconciliation? What do you have to lose? Linda F. nearly lost her health. If you did seek to reconcile the past, what might you gain?

 Plain *Truth*

Good nutrition and health care are readily at hand [for the Amish]. Years of physical labor and exercise have kept the body active. When health fails, relatives and friends come to visit frequently. There is no stigma attached to being sick. In case of financial need, either the relatives or the church will pay unmet medical bills.[5]

The Sugarcreek Scandal

Christ is our fortress, patience our weapon of defense, and the Word of God our sword.

Amish proverb

Clara and Walter T. share a tradition that has lasted as long as their fifty-three-year-old marriage: each evening, they sit on the back porch of their home to watch the sun set behind the hills. This summer twilight is particularly beautiful—hues of orange and red illuminate the clouds that hang in the sky. "Tomorrow," Walter says, "should be glorious."

This couple, gentle and kind and loving, has seen many days that have been glorious, and some—especially recently—that have been less than glorious. Their great-grandson, Luke, was born in 2009 with a genetic enzyme deficiency. Treatments help to stabilize his condition, but he will always need special care. Medical bills for Luke have run so high that the local community held an auction in May 2010 to help pay them off. "They hoped to raise forty thousand dollars," Walter said, "and they ended up raising twice that."

Yet there were still outstanding medical bills for Luke, as well as ongoing ones. Walter and Clara decided to cash out an investment they had made a few years earlier with an investment company, A&M Investors, to chip in for Luke's medical costs. A&M Investors was a safe, steady fund run by Monroe Beachy, a trusted Mennonite among the Plain People in the eastern Ohio area. A&M gave a better return than the banks, and Monroe assured investors that he only invested in low-risk government bonds. "Many in our church had invested with Monroe," Clara said. "They felt confident that their money was safe, but I never felt right about it."

"She never did," Walter echoed. "I should've listened." He leaned over and squeezed Clara's wrinkled hand.

"It just seemed too good to be true," she said.

Her instincts were right. In late June 2010, Walter called A&M Investors to withdraw his money, but no one answered the phone or returned his calls. Finally, Walter went to the office, found it dark and empty, with a notice on the door that said A&M Investors was closed and under investigation. Walter soon learned that Monroe Beachy had filed for bankruptcy because he had lost half of his clients' invested money. "Turns out he had been investing in risky dot-com stocks," Walter said matter-of-factly.

Clara frowned. "Risky on-the-line stocks!"

"Online," Walter whispered. "Internet, she means to say."

"No one in our church would want their money going to the internet," she added.

"She's right. We never would've put money into those kinds of investments, had we known."

111

But nobody did know, except Monroe Beachy. According to an article in *USA Today*, more than 2,700 people lost over $16 million because of A&M's fraud; the average investor lost about $13,000.[1] Clara and Walter lost over $20,000.

Religious leaders began a campaign to reverse the bankruptcy, to settle the matter out of court, but a bankruptcy judge rejected the plea. The refusal didn't deter the Amish. They kept plowing ahead, taking what they could into their own hands to avoid pursuing claims in court, which violates their faith. Donations were gathered to reimburse the Plain investors.

A non-Amish woman from Sugarcreek said that a number of local Amish didn't want this story to "explode in the press" (her words). "There are a lot of Amish millionaires in Holmes County," she said. "There's a lot of money in this county. They took up a collection to reimburse the Amish who had lost money in A&M. They didn't want people to look at the Amish and think it seemed like Amish would cheat Amish. They wanted to keep it very hush-hush."

So, of course, the scandal made national headline news, including an article in the *New York Times*.[2]

Clara said it was a terrible time for her community. "A lot of our friends lost money. I have some widow friends who lost money they were counting on. But the church took care of everyone and asked us to forgive Monroe."

In June 2012, two years after he had filed bankruptcy for A&M Investors, Monroe Beachy, age seventy-eight, was sentenced to six and a half years in prison after pleading no contest to the charges of mail fraud. The prosecutor had asked for the maximum term—twenty years. He wanted Beachy to get retributive justice, to receive his "due." In fact, wrote the authors of *Amish Grace*, "getting our due might be the most widely shared value in our hyperconsumerist culture. In such a world, forgiveness goes against the grain. In their own way, the Amish have constructed cultures that go against that grain."[3]

A response of extending forgiveness is part of that culture.

Clara and Walter had known Monroe Beachy for years and trusted him with their saved earnings. In return, he lied to them and sent statements with falsified figures. Could they truly forgive the man who had misused money they wanted to use for their great-grandson's special needs?

"Monroe Beachy was just a man," Clara said. "He made mistakes, like we all do. But our trust wasn't in him. It's in God. We trust and believe that God is taking care of us." She lifted her thin shoulders in a shrug. "It was only money. No one will miss it. But if we held on to bitterness, *that* would be remembered."

What if the church hadn't reimbursed the investors? Would forgiveness have come as easily for Clara and Walter? "It might have taken a little longer," Walter said, "but it still would have arrived."

 ## REFLECTIONS ON PEACEMAKING

> Money is complicated baggage. Most of us place enormous value on it—wanting more of it, accumulating it, trusting in it to always be there to provide for us. There's an old saying that goes like this: "The world stands on three things: on money, on money, and on money." Clara would disagree. Why was she able to let go of bitterness toward A&M Investors?

"If we held on to bitterness, *that* would be remembered," Clara said. Many physical problems can and will eventually get fixed. But not our inner problems. What will others remember about you? What do you want to be remembered for?

"Monroe Beachy was just a man," Clara said. Why was her perception about Monroe Beachy's flawed humanity a healthy one? Where did she place her security?

Describe a person you know who has chosen not to forgive, but instead has held a grudge for months or even years. How would you characterize him or her? Novelist Frederick Buechner said it best: "To lick your wounds, to smack your lips over grievances long past, to roll over your tongue the prospect of bitter confrontations still to come, to savor to the last toothsome morsel both the pain you are given and the pain you are giving back—in many ways it is a feast fit for a king. The chief drawback is that what you are wolfing down is yourself."[4]

Plain *Truth*

Amish run 9,000 companies across North America, from the family-operated roadside stands to multimillion-dollar furniture dealers and manufacturers. They've seen five-year survival rates upwards of 90 percent. Amish millionaires, once unheard of, are hardly uncommon nowadays (though you certainly wouldn't think it by the way they dress or the vehicles they drive). One Amish business owner put it well. Alvin Hershberger runs a flourishing furniture shop in Ohio's Holmes County community. Alvin is gregarious and easygoing, but clearly serious and committed to his business. He also happens to be a minister in his church, home to a high proportion of thriving businesspeople like him. "If I'm a millionaire, you won't notice it," Alvin said. "If I make $50,000 a year, it's still the same. It's what I do with it."[5]

Blessing Our Circumstances

---

*The person who forgives does more for himself
than for anyone else.*

Amish proverb

Spending a childhood in Kentucky, surrounded by horses,
was just the environment to shape a young animal lover
like Jacinda Gore. Raised in a Beachy Amish (a split
from the Old Order Amish) home, Jacinda was an excellent
rider by the age of ten, had a chicken-and-egg business, was
learning sign language so that she could be an interpreter for
the deaf one day—and then she planned to marry a rancher
and live in Wyoming, and raise eleven children (after all, she
would need the children to help run the ranch). Oh, and she
thought about becoming an evangelist for her Beachy Amish
church too. Jacinda was a girl who had her life planned out.
Hopes, goals, and dreams.

When Jacinda was fourteen, she started to have painful
kidney stones and was diagnosed with kidney disease. For
the next four years, she was in and out of the hospital with

new symptoms that brought new diagnoses from new specialists. Sherry, Jacinda's mother, put all her energy and financial resources into finding cures and treatments to help her daughter. "I followed up any little lead," Sherry said. "One referral led to another and another. I used to think there was nothing worse than losing a child to death. Now I think the worst thing is watching a child suffer."[1]

When Jacinda was seventeen, the doctors made a definitive diagnosis: she had an esophageal brain stem glioma, a tumor in the brain that is slow growing and inoperable. "At seventeen, the treatment for Jacinda was changed from curative to palliative through hospice," Sherry said.

For two and a half years, Sherry felt she was constantly grieving—for a death that hadn't happened yet. A small woman, Sherry's weight ballooned up to 218 pounds. "It was all emotional eating," she said. "I was grief stricken. As Jacinda's disease had progressed, I was grieving every loss in her life. She didn't get to play volleyball with the youth or marry that rancher and live in Wyoming. I was stuck in grief, and I felt I had every right to cry. I lived in a fog, just waiting for it to clear. I was waiting for things to get better. And they never did." Sherry supported her family by cleaning houses. "I know I was let go of several cleaning jobs because I was so grief stricken. I was not a joy to be around.

"I finally got to the breaking point," Sherry continued. "Even though this experience has been terrible, I have a responsibility to share my grief with God. And when I started to do that—to pray while I cried—then the healing began." Sherry's favorite Bible passage is from the book of Habakkuk:

> Although the fig tree shall not blossom, neither shall fruit be in the vines; the labour of the olive shall fail, and the fields

shall yield no meat; the flock shall be cut off from the fold, and there shall be no herd in the stalls:

Yet I will rejoice in the LORD, I will joy in the God of my salvation. (Hab. 3:17–18 KJV)

"Since that breaking point, I have learned that healing begins much sooner if I can turn things over to God as soon as possible. I still grieve; it is griefworthy. It's only natural. But God is supernatural. The healing begins as soon as I let go. It doesn't all go away right away, but it starts. And I know I will hurt longer if I don't turn my grief over to God." As part of her healing process, Sherry has lost fifty-six pounds. "I realized I had choices. I had to let go. I had to accept what I couldn't change. I was able to say to God, this is yours. Jacinda is yours. I am yours."

Jacinda is now twenty-four. Her life is filled with continual loss and constant suffering. Every day is a battle. "Our battle has switched from fighting disease," Sherry said, "to a spiritual battle to remain faithful. I often ask God, 'How much more can she take?' And God answers, 'More.' It's hard. I hang on to Revelation 2:10." ("Though He slay me, yet will I trust in Him," KJV.)

Through this long journey, Sherry has learned a great deal about human nature. "My love for others is much better when I see them through God's perspective. I have a lot of compassion. But in another way, I have less tolerance for people who are whiners. Really, I think? You think your week is wrecked over *that*?"

Turning to writing, for Sherry, has become part of the process of healing. "And God has blessed me," she said. Now living in Pinecraft, Florida, Sherry has published two cookbooks, *Simply Delicious Amish* and *Me, Myself and Pie* (Zondervan), started a quarterly food magazine called *Cooking & Such: Adventures in Plain Living*, writes a monthly Scribe letter for *The Budget*, has been interviewed by *National Geographic* for a television special, as well as PBS's *American Experience*, and is working on more books. "But I'm a mother first," Sherry said. "A caregiver second. A writer third. It's true that I have had to stop my work to care for Jacinda's health emergencies, but it's never been a question for me. I stay right where my heart is."

Sherry said that everything rests on her relationship with God. "If I didn't have Him, I'd have nothing. Everything is insignificant to my relationship with God. Invite Him to share in your pain. Healing begins instantly. It might not be over, but it begins."

The Lord called Jacinda Gore home on Friday, February 6, 2015. "Precious in the sight of the LORD is the death of his saints" (Psalm 116:15 KJV).

 ## REFLECTIONS ON PEACEMAKING

"Though we feel we have a right to grieve," Sherry Gore said, "the sooner you share it with God, the better. Don't keep it to yourself. Turn it right over." What is causing you grief today? How can you invite God into the conversation?

Heaven, to Sherry, is "as real as if I can reach out and touch it." How does that perspective affect your thinking?

"I have learned by experience that the longer I hang on to this," Sherry said, "the longer it will take before healing starts. The length of time to grieve is up to me." Have you ever thought about grief and healing as being under your control?

Plain *Truth*

The Beachy Amish church split from the Old Order Amish church in 1927 over the controversy of allowing automobile ownership. The Beachy Amish are nicknamed for their leader, Bishop Moses M. Beachy. In contrast to the Old Order Amish, the Beachy Amish have meetinghouses, Sunday school, and a Bible school for young adults, and most support missionary work. Social shunning and excommunication are used less frequently, and accompanying bans are even more rare.

A Four-Hundred-Year-Old Bible

―――――――― ⌀ ――――――――

The smallest vengeance poisons the soul.

Amish proverb

―――――――――――――――――――――――――――――――――

ount up the Bibles in your home. Most likely, there are quite a few, of assorted translations, varied bindings—hardback or paperback—font size, study notes, maps, and illustrations. Reading the Bible in your own language is a luxury few would consider to be a privilege. But it hasn't always been that way.

Five hundred years ago, in Zurich, Switzerland, a Bible written in the common vernacular might have been legally confiscated from your home—if you had a conflict with the State church over the theology of adult baptism versus infant baptism, and especially if it was a Froschau edition of the Bible.

During the turbulent period of the Protestant Reformation, a man named Christoph Froschauer ran a printing shop in Zurich, Switzerland. From 1525 to 1529, he labored to produce parts of the New Testament in German, using both the available translations of Martin Luther and the translations of Huldrych Zwingli. An outspoken pastor, Zwingli was responsible for promoting the Protestant Reformation in Switzerland. As more books of the Bible were translated, Froschauer started to work on the Old Testament. In 1531, Froschauer printed a single volume of the entire Bible, Old Testament and New Testament. At the time, the Froschau Bible, containing more than two hundred illustrations, was (and continues to be) known as a masterpiece of printing.

Anabaptist leaders were eager to possess their own Froschau Bible—paying as much as four times the going value. Literate laypersons sought black-market copies of the Bible. It was considered to be a priceless treasure. While this translation held translated parts by Martin Luther, most of it was in the dialect of the common Swiss people.

Four hundred and fifty years later, the Froschau printing office, called Zur Froschau, was still in existence. Sabine Aschmann, a young girl in Zurich, knew the shop well. Her father owned the Froschau printing shop from 1960 to 1980.

When Aschmann became ordained as a pastor at a Reformed church, she acquired a 1548 Froschau Bible as a souvenir of Zur Froschau, her family's business.[1] "As a child I was fascinated by this history," Aschmann said, "and that was the reason I wanted to possess an old Froschauerbible. For me it was a remembrance of the printing office of my father and a connection to the Zurich of Zwingli, the town where I studied theology. I loved this Bible very much because of its language: old German with Swiss-German tinge.

"The Anabaptists esteemed the Froschau Bibles very much," Aschmann continued. "Especially the edition of 1536." She bought her 1548 Froschau Bible from the library of the

Schauffhauser Ministerium (the union of pastors of the church of the canton of Schauffhausen). "The Bible had belonged to a late pastor with the name A. Haberlin in the twentieth century. That's all I know about the history of this Bible."

Sort of. There's actually a legend attached to Aschmann's 1548 Froschau Bible, but she said it can't be verified. As the story goes, in the sixteenth century, this Bible belonged to an Anabaptist family named Eberly. The Bible was stolen from Eberly and confiscated by the government of Schauffhausen during that brutal wave of Anabaptist persecution.

As the calendar turned to a new century, a Swiss Reformed pastor named Geri Keller felt a growing burden to reconcile past persecution. Keller organized the "Heal Our Land" conference that was held in Winterthur, Switzerland, on May 1–4, 2003. Over eight hundred attended, including Swiss Reformed pastors and Anabaptists from all over the world. Thirty Swiss Reformed pastors, dressed in their clerical robes, publicly washed the feet of every Anabaptist leader, tearfully asking for and receiving forgiveness. Speakers representing the State Reformed church acknowledged the wrongs done to the Anabaptists and asked for forgiveness. The Anabaptists repented of attitudes toward the State church and sought freedom from the effects of persecution.

Sabine Aschmann attended the conference. During the sessions, it occurred to her how much the Anabaptists had lost in the sixteenth century because of the persecution by the state church. "My forefathers in the reformed confession had robbed the Anabaptists of their native country," she said. Many Anabaptists fled Switzerland because of the persecution. "Therefore it was not possible for them to take part in the reformation process. They were not accepted and they were divorced from the inheritance of reformation. I realized very clearly that the outcome of the reformation, for example, the German translation of the Bible . . . the word of God doesn't only belong to us, but also to the Anabaptists."

Aschmann felt very moved, very affected by what she had discovered about the troubled history between the Anabaptists and the Swiss Reformed church. "So it happened to me during the conference that I began to wish to give a prophetic sign for reconciliation," Aschmann said. "I wanted to give my Froschauerbible away. I spoke about this with Pfarrer Geri Keller. He agreed with me. At the end of the conference, my Bible was given into the hands of the Lancaster delegation."

The unexpected gift of the Bible made international news. It was a generous act on many levels—both monetarily (the rare Froschau Bible is worth quite a bit of money) and symbolically. It became heralded as tangible evidence of the significant work of reconciliation.

"After the Conference of Winterthur," Aschmann said, "there were many commemorations in all of Switzerland. [Acknowledgments of the process of reconciliation between the government and church of each Canton and the Anabaptists who had been persecuted in that specific region.] For me it was obvious that in the invisible world something had broken up and a wave of reconciliation had come over Switzerland. Reconciliation and forgiveness bring spiritual change. They bring a visible change in the present."

REFLECTIONS ON PEACEMAKING

Does it really make a difference to seek reconciliation for events that happened five hundred years ago? "While we cannot change the past," Lloyd Hoover said in an interview with Winterthur Conference attendee Joanne Hess Siegrist, "we can change the way we think of ourselves in the present, and create a new identity for the future."[2]

Another Winterthur Conference attendee noted, "This conference also made me realize more than ever before how we need to address the divisions within our own denomination here in our own country. How might the Lord work reconciliation here in America? There are various Mennonite groups that do not worship together, although we claim a common faith tradition. What about relationships between Anabaptists of today and other denominations? Can we reach out to other faith traditions with respect and affirm our common faith in Christ without imposing our beliefs upon each other?" Those questions aren't applicable solely to Anabaptists but to all of those who profess the Christian faith. What are your thoughts about those important questions?

There are other examples of historic after-the-fact reconciliations: the Truth and Reconciliation Commission held in Cape Town, South Africa, in 1996, for one, held after the abolition of Apartheid. What kind of impact does an event like that have on the world? On the church? What about on you, personally?

Plain *Truth*

Threatened by the rapid spread of Anabaptist groups, civil and religious authorities commissioned "Anabaptist hunters" to hunt down the dissenters. The first martyr, Felix Mantz, was killed in 1527 by drowning. Over several decades, nearly 2,500 Anabaptists were burned at the stake, drowned in rivers, starved in prisons, or lost their heads to the executioner's swords. And still the movement continued to grow.

Through My Tears

Forgiveness is not a matter of what we remember,
but how we remember.

Amish proverb

It was a warm spring night in New Philadelphia, Ohio, an idyllic pastoral town deep in the heart of Amish country—Holmes County. Becki Reiser (who isn't Amish) had given her seventeen-year-old daughter, Liz, a senior in high school, permission to stay overnight at her best friend's home after church youth group.

Becki felt a little hitch in her gut as she said good-bye to Liz. It was unusual to let her spend a school night at a friend's house, but this was the spring of her senior year. Her grades were good, her life was on track. Why not give her a little breathing room?

So Becki set aside that little hitch and went about helping her three younger children, all boys, finish up homework and get to bed.

At 3:30 in the morning, Becki and her husband, Jeff, heard a knock at the door. It was a police officer, asking if they knew where their daughter was. Brandi, Liz's friend, had been found down by the river. The officer had no information about Liz's whereabouts. He told them he would call if there was any information.

At that point, Becki and Jeff sat in the living room. Praying, waiting, praying, waiting. Becki heard the crinkle of turning pages and knew that her husband was reading his Bible.

"What do you know?" she asked him.

Jeff lifted his eyes from the Bible to look at her. "We need to go to the hospital at six a.m."

Becki and Jeff went to the hospital—still without any information about their daughter. When they arrived, the police were there. They had found Liz.

Liz and Brandi had left the church and stopped by a video store. A man approached them and said he needed a ride. Normally, Liz and Brandi didn't offer rides in the car to strangers, but they both felt that it should be okay. After all, there were two of them, the man needed help, and they had been raised to help others in need.

This time, it wasn't okay.

On the outside, the stranger seemed normal, a father of three children who lived in the area. Inside, he was unhinged, determined to kill someone that night. He gave Brandi and Liz confusing directions, until they asked him to leave the car. At that point, he took out a gun and ordered Brandi to drive to a field. He handcuffed her to the steering wheel and took Liz out in the field, where he raped her, slashed her, then killed her. He returned to the car to assault Brandi. She fought him off, and as he tried to choke her, she pretended she was dead. He tossed her off a fifteen-foot bridge into a river, where she floated, trying to appear lifeless, until she saw him leave. She was able to get to the road and flag help from a passing car.

The detective told this horrifying story to the Reisers. The first words out of Jeff's mouth were: "We forgive the killer."

Becki nodded in agreement. "It was instantaneous," she said. "It was complete."

Earlier, while Jeff had been reading the Bible and praying, he asked God to tell him where Liz was. His eyes locked on the Bible phrase "Blessed are those who mourn, for they will be comforted" (Matt. 5:4).

At that moment, in his heart, Jeff knew. His daughter was gone. She was with the Lord.

The stranger, Matthew Vaca, was apprehended and confessed to the crime. Becki and Jeff pursued conviction. Their forgiveness did not mean that they would have waved away the need for this man to be incarcerated for his crimes, as well as the need to keep society safe from such an evildoer.

Nor did it mean that they did not grieve deeply for Liz and continue to grieve deeply. They miss their daughter. Their sons miss their sister. A week after Liz's death, her college acceptance letter arrived in the mail. "That was . . . a hard moment," Becki said, her voice breaking.

Recently, Becki self-published a book about their journey. In it, she wrote a letter to her daughter:

"Life has definitely changed. Some days I don't like it much. My heart hurts, and I just don't want to do anything. I want to sit in the house with the curtains closed and not talk to anyone, not clean anything, not cook, and just feel sorry for myself. I get angry because my life was drastically altered because of a crazed man with murder in his heart. I would like to slap him some days. And other days I wish that he wouldn't exist anymore. There are days when I wish we had pushed for the death penalty. Why would we have to push for it? I must confess too that there are days when I would be okay if I simply didn't wake up. No more worries. No more pressure to be the right kind of person. No more feeling like a part of me is missing, and no more throbbing pain. I am tired. But I always remember your father's words, and we forgive the man who did this."[1]

Jeff's choice that day led his family into healing and wholeness. Becki and Jeff have created a ministry of grief counseling and forgiveness called Through My Tears.

Their ability to forgive, they believe, was God-given. "It was easier to forgive that murderer than it has been to forgive someone for a careless or hurtful remark," Becki said.

For a long time after Liz's death, Becki thought if she had just listened to the hitch in her gut, if she had just said no to the overnight at Brandi's house, *then* her daughter would still be alive. Does she still feel that way? "No. I believe God has ordained each person's days on earth. I believe Liz's life was complete."

 REFLECTIONS ON PEACEMAKING

Becki said that it was easier to forgive the murderer than it has been to forgive someone for a careless or hurtful remark. It seems so contrary to our nature, but sometimes it is easier to forgive for a big offense than to forgive someone for something small or petty. Why do you think that is true? Have you ever had a similar response?

God doesn't intend for us to forgive all on our own. Becki said that she never would have thought she was capable of this kind of forgiveness. "Our ability to forgive Matthew Vaca came from God Himself," she writes in *Through My Tears*. "Complete forgiveness is God's job."[2] How does Becki's experience with forgiveness aid your own process?

"Without forgiving the perpetrator, Jeff and I and those around us would be buried in anger and pain and a need for vengeance. But forgiveness brings relief. I can sum up forgiveness in one word: Freedom."[3] What do you think Becki meant by that?

Becki and Jeff knew that forgiving their enemy was important for their own spiritual consequences. "God has surely taken the root of vengeance from me," Jeff said. "I know full well that the Lord is protecting my soul. The peace I experience is a gift given me by Jesus, one that will last my lifetime."[4]

 Plain *Truth*

"The Amish answer to the problem of evil is neither airtight nor entirely consistent from one person to the next. Their unwavering confidence in God's providence inclines them toward the belief that God sometimes allows evil things to happen for purposes that are not immediately obvious but are part of some greater long-term good in God's big picture plan. Still others argue that humans will never fully understand why bad things happen under God's watch. Nonetheless, their unwavering confidence in God's providence inclines them to leave many questions unresolved."[5]

Rachel's Stand

Standing your ground is easier when you are grounded in God's Word.

Amish proverb

Rachel Y. had one of the hardest roads for a woman to travel to forgiveness. She was only nine years old when her father molested her for the first time. She thought such behavior was normal. "I thought every dad did those things to his daughters," she said. "I thought it was part of their life too. I learned to accept it. That's the way it was. That was my whole idea of a dad." She believed the lies that her father told her because she didn't know otherwise.

Rachel was right in the middle of ten children—five boys and five girls—in an Old Order Amish family in a large settlement in Indiana. She didn't dwell on the abuse. Most of it, she blocked out of her mind.

"My dad had a lot of anger issues. Whenever he wanted to have sex with me," she paused, "if I didn't, the whole day, he would take it out on the whole family. Especially Mom. I let him have it so he would be happy. I didn't want Mom hurt. But that's how he knew he would get what he wanted."

When Rachel became a teenager, she started to see that connections other girls had with their fathers weren't like the one she had. "It looked like they really loved their dad. I got to the point where I realized, this isn't right."

Rachel's father was sly. "He made me believe that Mom knew all about it. She had kids to take care of. She wasn't able to take care of him. So that was my job. I hated thinking about it."

If Rachel ever said she might tell someone, her father threatened suicide. "And then it would all be my fault." He even threatened, in anger, to kill her if she said anything.

Secrecy and fear are key components of perpetuating abuse. Abusers know that secrecy allows abuse to thrive.

The dynamics of Rachel's household added to the confusion. As hard as it is to conceive of goodness and kindness in a man who sexually abused his daughters, Rachel said her father had a kind side. He was a gift giver, and he liked to talk.

By contrast, her mother spoke very little, and when she did speak, it was short. "She was noncommunicative," Rachel said. "That's what her family had been like." For example, her mother never discussed menstruation with her. "You don't say the word 'sex.' For the Amish, you don't hear those words." Fortunately, Rachel had older sisters to talk to and ask questions. "When Mom found out I had started my cycle, she asked me, 'Why didn't you tell me?' I told her, 'Well, why didn't you tell me?'"

Children from dysfunctional families and families with poor communication are at significant risk for seduction. Rachel's dad talked about all kinds of things. "Too much.

Dad started talking to me about sex at age eight. He was telling me stuff I should never have known. I was told in a wrong way. It was so turned around."

At fourteen, Rachel was ready to put an end to the abuse. She waited until a time when she was alone with her mother. "'Mom,' I said, 'I need to tell you something. Dad does something to me.'"

Her mother had no idea the abuse had been going on. "It's hard to believe she didn't, but she was shocked. She said, 'Oh my goodness. Are you serious?' She asked me some questions to make sure I was telling the truth. That evening, she went over to the bishop and talked to him."

Rachel's father was put under the Bann. "He was shunned for one or two weeks. He apologized to the church. Then everything went back to normal—except that everybody knew. Dad grew even more angry. He knew we were in control. He had a lot of temper tantrums. It was something he couldn't control himself. The devil was so much inside him. You could tell the devil had hold of him."

When Rachel's little sister turned three, she felt she had to do more. "I didn't want her to go through the same thing I went through. So I told my older brother about what Dad was doing. He said, 'We've got to turn him in.'"

The bishop called for a family meeting—similar to an intervention. "We told my father that he had to go somewhere, he had to get counseling, or we would turn him in to the police." She paused. "He wasn't sorry for what he had done. He was sorry we told. He didn't repent like we had hoped."

His response, or lack of one, falls in line with pedophiles. It's typical for them to have a stunning lack of conscience. Though pedophiles vary greatly, they are able to successfully hide their activities for a very long time. They can spend their entire lives rationalizing and justifying their behavior, proclaiming innocence.

Rachel and her brother went ahead and notified the police. Charges were filed against her father. Eventually, he was sent to jail for three and a half years. "It would have been longer, but the Amish preachers and bishop had written letters on his behalf. They had said that he has accepted Christ and asked for forgiveness. They told the judge that they would not let any abuse continue."

That, Rachel felt, was a mistake. The church leaders didn't understand the magnitude of the problem they were dealing with.

Invisible wounds are the hardest ones to heal. While Rachel's father was in prison, she realized that she had a great deal of bitterness harbored within her. She moved out of her childhood home. "I couldn't go anywhere without people coming up to me and bringing it up. Everybody knew everything. I needed to get out. I didn't want to talk about it. I moved out to breathe. I wanted a fresh new start."

She moved near one of her brothers, who had left the Old Order Amish church and attended a nondenominational church. "He wanted me to go to church. I wasn't ready. I was afraid to call myself a Christian. I was tired of working on my soul. Everyone kept telling me that I needed to forgive. Well, I was sick and tired of it."

But her brother kept persisting in inviting her, and finally Rachel did go to church. She heard the message that Jesus loved her, no matter what. It didn't matter what she had been through. "That was the time that I accepted Christ."

Rachel started to feel some pity for her father. "When he was off in prison, I felt sorry for him. I knew how kind he could be. But he's still not sorry, not the way he should be.

That's my daily struggle. That's what I have a hard time forgiving."

Currently, Rachel's father is out of prison and under parole. He lives separately from Rachel's mother and is not allowed to visit with the family unless he has been invited. Everyone, including the Amish leaders, now wishes her father had spent more time in prison. "You'd think they would have wanted to keep him away from the little sister at home. We are going to be sure nothing is going to happen to her. We have enough support to protect her."

Forgiveness doesn't necessarily restore the status quo, writes Gary Inrig in *The Risk of Forgiveness: What It Means to Forgive*. "Forgiveness isn't the same as reconciliation. Forgiveness clears the ledger; it does not instantly rebuild trust. Forgiveness is a given; reconciliation is earned. Forgiveness cancels debts; it does not eliminate all consequences. Reconciliation and forgiveness are related, but quite distinct."[1]

Today, Rachel's father is included in family gatherings. "We want to show him that we do forgive him. I have forgiven him. I'm even thankful for the way I grew up. I'm okay with the abuse I endured because I am stronger. I learned from it. I think it's important to take the bad things in our lives and learn from them.

"But will we let my father be with kids? Absolutely not. Trust may take the rest of our lives."

REFLECTIONS ON PEACEMAKING

What if Rachel had thrown in the towel with God—dismissed Him along with her father? The Enemy wants to keep people from knowing and trusting God. Certainly, childhood victimization is an effective deterrent. But Rachel turned to God for healing and found freedom from bitterness; she found the path to healing and wholeness.

Forgiveness is a journey, Dr. Dick Tibbits writes in *Forgive to Live*, and the deeper the wounds, the longer the journey. "But it is a journey that offers significant rewards along the way."[2] Rachel's father needed to go to jail. She needed to leave home to get healthy. There are points when an individual or a family needs to go beyond the home, beyond the community, to get professional help. What do you need to do to let go of your hurtful past?

One of the Enemy's great lies is to make a victim of child abuse believe that God betrayed her by permitting the abuse to occur. Scripture says otherwise: God is *never* the author of abuse. Clearly, God cares very deeply about each child and all that happens to them. He will avenge the abuse or victimization of children (Lam. 3:59; Zech. 2:8; Matt. 18:2–7). Beth Moore writes in her book *Breaking Free*, "No matter what atrocity has taken place in your family line, God can raise up a new generation of godly seed. Between every unfaithful generation and faithful generation is one person determined to change. You could be that link."[3]

Plain *Truth*

Many churches practice excommunication, but the use of shunning, a social avoidance, is unique to the Amish. Jakob Ammann, founder of the Amish, was a Swiss Anabaptist leader. He believed the Bible taught that excommunicated church members should be socially avoided. This idea originated from an early Anabaptist Confession of Faith. The Swiss Anabaptists, however, did not practice shunning. Jakob Ammann became embroiled in a dispute with Swiss Anabaptist leaders over this practice. Other issues were involved as well, but shunning was the decisive one that led the followers of Jakob Ammann to separate from the Swiss Anabaptists in 1693. Over the years, shunning continued to be a distinguishing mark of Amish practice.[4]

Grace Walked In

Dwight LeFever's father was a milk truck driver among the Amish in Pennsylvania. "Sometimes I would go along with my dad and play with the Amish kids," LeFever said. "They would come running when they saw the truck pull up the drive. They liked to ask if they could get chocolate milk out of the truck."

Unless you've grown up in dairy country, you might not realize how connected a milk truck driver is to a rural community. As connected as the mailman, the driver brings news and information to the Amish families along the routes. "Every other day, that truck comes barreling up the driveway to collect milk from dairies," LeFever said. "Families trust him."

Fast-forward to the morning of October 2, 2006. LeFever, now grown, married with children of his own, and a pastor at a small church, was at work in his church office when he heard rumblings about a shooting at an Amish schoolhouse, five or six miles away. "As the news accounts started to come in, we gathered for prayer. Many local guys at our church were EMTs, and we knew they might be first responders."

As the morning progressed, LeFever remembered a family from his previous church, the Welks, who lived close to where the school shooting was. He called Nadine Welk and left a message, thinking she might have some news.

A short time later, Nadine returned his call. "It was Charlie," Nadine said in a flat, stunned voice. She was referring to the milk truck driver who had gone into the schoolhouse that morning and shot ten little Amish girls. Charlie Roberts. Nadine's son-in-law.

LeFever left work immediately to go to the Welks' home. "We didn't have this kind of thing in seminary. How to respond to a high-level crisis. I wasn't sure what I would say or do, but I wanted to offer comfort and prayer.

"It was a chaotic situation. People were driving by the house. The Welks' home was in the epicenter of the situation." After several hours, LeFever drove over to the Robertses', whom he also knew from his previous church. "The family had gathered—Charlie's brothers, in-laws—trying to come to grips with this. It was so hard. There was a devastating pall. That's the best word to describe it—a pall, a heaviness. Here was the deepest heartache, mourning, and grief." After a few hours, they saw a lone Amish man come up to the house and knock on the door. They had no idea what he wanted or why he had come.

"We will forgive you," the Amish man told the Robertses. "It will be okay. We will find a way forward."

LeFever described that moment as hope being injected into the room. "Up to then, there was very little hope. So much hurt and uncertainty of what this would mean—on every level. For that man to humbly walk in and assure us that there will be, somehow, a tomorrow . . ." He paused, searching for the right words. "Well, it felt like grace walked in."

That moment, LeFever said, was the first of several turning points on the long road to healing for this hurting community. "The second one was Charlie's funeral, attended by thirty to forty Amish people, including direct relatives of the little girls who had been shot. I remember hearing an Amish grandmother say, 'We had to come.' You knew God's presence was there."

Another turning point came a month later. "At the Bart Township Fire Station, there was a time of sharing for the Nickel Mines families, the Welks, and the Robertses. I opened in prayer and read Romans 8:39: 'Neither height nor depth, nor anything else in all creation, will be able to separate us from the love of God that is in Christ Jesus our Lord.' There were a lot of tears, even from Amish grandfathers who were normally so stoic and so strong. A rare show of emotion." LeFever said an Amish man brought a gift for the wife of Charlie Roberts—a hand-carved crib for her daughter's baby doll. "I thought to myself, 'Here it is again. This light. Another shift. Another shift.' They all add up."

LeFever felt that the Amish offered forgiveness in a way that was unnatural to human nature. Most of us, he said, want to get back what is owed to us. "Forgiveness is an emotional thing. It hurts. It aches. It's hard to go beyond what we feel. But if we let our emotions guide us, they'll never get us there. The Amish seem to understand that. They take to heart Ephesians 4:32: 'Be kind and compassionate to one another, forgiving each other, just as in Christ God forgave you.' They get that. They've been forgiven much, and they believe to withhold forgiveness is sin (Matt. 6:14–15).

"There's a Greek word, *aphesis*. It means to release. You release someone from hurt, like an act of surrender. Usually, if you're under pressure, something is held over you. Guilt. You can't escape it. But when it's released—you have . . . *room!* To catch your breath, to allow God to start the healing. It gets to the heart of forgiveness."

And the healing process is still going on. "But these families, all of them, they're not staying stuck. They're moving forward. This isn't how it usually happens. This is the power of forgiveness. This is God's work."

 ## Reflections on Peacemaking

Whenever LeFever is asked to speak about the Nickel Mines shooting, he closes the talk with these comments: "How does the lane of Nickel Mines intersect with your road? What does it mean to you? Everybody has something or somebody to forgive. Everybody has a need to be forgiven. It's a universal issue." How would you respond to those questions?

LeFever keeps in touch with the Roberts and Welk families. He said that Charlie Roberts's mother, Terri, visits with the most seriously wounded Amish girl regularly. She reads to this little girl, brushes her hair, spends time with her. She's consistently reached out to her for years. "We can facilitate healing in others by offering forgiveness," LeFever said. Terri's desire to connect with this little girl and her family comes not from guilt but out of the grace that was extended to her. What are some practical ways you can show someone you forgive them?

Plain *Truth*

In writing the book *Amish Grace: How Forgiveness Transcended Tragedy*, the authors discovered that forgiveness is embedded more deeply in the Amish life than they had suspected. "That realization inspired us to listen more closely for the religious heartbeat that sustains their entire way of life. This pulse, which often goes unnoticed, is more fundamental to the Amish way than the buggies and bonnets that receive so much attention. Strong but subtle, quiet yet persistent, this heartbeat is Amish spirituality."[1]

Two Lives

—— ⌒⌒ ——

When all we have left is God, we have all that we need.

Amish proverb

The first thing you notice about Terri Roberts is her joy. It's infectious. She is a woman who has not only battled stage 3 breast cancer but has also confronted a heartbreak that no mother should ever have to face, and yet she radiates joy.

Terri's son, Charles Roberts, was the gunman who shot ten little Amish girls in the Nickel Mines schoolhouse, killing five and injuring five. "That first night," Terri said, "I didn't know if I wanted to wake up. 'God,' I said, 'this is so ugly. If you can do anything to redeem this ugliness, you can do *anything.*'"[1]

Without a doubt, Terri feels, God has brought redeeming moments out of an unspeakable tragedy. Healing hasn't come all at once, but in small steps. "The day of the shooting, my husband sat in a chair and hung his head. He hadn't lifted his head all afternoon. An Amish man named Henry—I call him my angel in black—he came to our home and stayed with us. When he got ready to leave, he put his hand on my husband's shoulder and said that he forgave us. At that, my husband lifted his head and eyes. It was the first glimmer of any hope that we would get over this. It would take a long time, but we would heal."

The expressions of sincere forgiveness offered by the Amish set into motion the process of healing in Terri and Chuck. "Would we have come through this without the forgiving response of the Amish? Yes, but it made our ability to heal and move forward so much easier. For us, there was no bitterness from the Amish. The overall response was forgiveness and acceptance."

Terri deserves some credit too. She didn't avoid the fallout from this tragedy, but walked right into it. In January of 2007, only three months after the shooting, Terri started to visit each family who had a child hurt or killed in the shooting. "God put it in me. We are connected to these families in a very deep, deep way. I wanted to see how they were doing." She smiled at the memory. "That first meeting—to say it felt scary would be putting it mildly."

But the first meeting and then the second one, Terri said, were all that they could possibly be. The welcome and warmth from the Amish families "drenched our souls."

Terri believes that the ability of the Amish to gracefully weather sorrow and grief has to do with their concept of community. "It's so much stronger than anything I've ever seen. They are there to pour love on you, to walk alongside you. They've got something so right. Not everything, but they do community right."

Another aspect to the Amish that she noticed in those visits was their candor. "In one home, the dad was very honest and forthright. He told me many additional details. It was hard, it held pain—but I was glad he did it. In asking about details, he was bringing out the underlying emotion that went with it. Some things were hard to hear, but I was so glad it wasn't hidden."

Encouraged by the positive outcome of those visits, Terri decided to host a backyard picnic for the families. It was such a positive afternoon that Terri soon hosted a tea party for the little Amish girls. And that led to meeting with the mothers, regularly and privately, for times of sharing and support. "We go deep!" she said, a smile in her voice. "The Amish do move on, but not everyone moves on at the same rate. Some of the women were getting pushed to move on before they were ready. Our time together has become a place to share our pain."

During the first gathering of mothers, Terri asked each one to share the hardest part of her healing and a highlight of her healing. One mother, Mary Liz, spoke of her daughter, Rosanna, only six years old, who was severely injured in the shooting. She said that the mothers who had lost a daughter were getting consoled. The mothers of the daughters who healed were able to share with each other. But her daughter had not healed.

Months earlier, at the backyard picnic she hosted, Terri had held Rosanna in her lap and felt a yearning to connect to her. After the meeting with the mothers, Terri asked if she could visit each week to help with Rosanna. Mary Liz instantly said yes. "It was amazing to me," Terri said, "to be invited into their home. But those first two weeks, I came home and sat in my driveway and the tears did not stop. I cried and cried.

Finally, I cried out to God. 'Lord,' I said, 'I felt You were calling me to this. I can't be an emotional basket case each week. I'm no good to them or me.' After that, I have never been as overcome as I was in those first two weeks. It was all God's doing. It had nothing to do with me or my strength."

Rosanna is now thirteen. Terri continues to visit her weekly, providing care and companionship. "It's amazing to see who she has blossomed into. Rosanna's brother told me recently that it's been so helpful to them that I've been a part of their lives. That is the overall consensus, that I've been a real encouragement to them." She stopped abruptly, tears choking her voice. "It touches my heart. I'm a constant reminder of what happened to their daughter at the hand of my son. My son was responsible for that child's situation."

Today, Terri speaks around the world about healing and forgiveness, for body and soul. Her life is not defined by the tragedy of the Nickel Mines story. "It's a piece of my life, but by God's grace, I've been able to move forward. To move to the next step is the important part." Can anybody do this? "Yes! Anybody can. This was my story, but we all have a story to tell. We all have things tearing at our heart. The darkest part is not your whole story. God can redeem the day. His redemptive power is amazing."

❖ REFLECTIONS ON PEACEMAKING

In Terri's speaking engagements, she encourages people to get past the event that is controlling them, their thoughts, their life. To move forward. "The darkest part is not your whole story." How do you get there? "Through the reality of divine power," Terri said. Have you witnessed God's divine power at work in someone's darkest part? How has He worked in your darkest part?

Terri's regular pattern of spending time with Rosanna is a way of showing enduring love, of reminding the family that she isn't going away, that she's here and walking alongside them. How does that kind of practical help facilitate healing?

One positive outcome of the Nickel Mines incident is a greater openness for the Amish to seek and receive counseling. "Traditionally, they haven't reached outside for professional help," Terri said. "But that seems to be changing." How have you seen God bring good out of circumstances that seem hopeless?

 ## Plain *Truth*

"For the Amish, the Lord's Prayer is *the* prayer. Many Amish people reflect on it several times a day, even more on church days. From an Amish perspective, trying to improve on the Lord's Prayer would reflect a proud heart. This simple, ancient prayer is therefore the key to Amish spirituality."[2]

Shielding Marie

Let your life story be for God's glory.

Amish proverb

It was one of the hardest days of Marie Roberts's life. She was in a car, heading to the cemetery where her husband, Charlie Roberts, would be laid to rest. Buried.

The police said no media would be allowed on church property. But as the car drove into the cemetery where Marie Roberts's husband would be buried, she was shocked. "As we came around the corner, it was such a startling time for me. It was the first time I'd been back to Nickel Mines. The first time I'd seen how intrusive the media was into this community. Reporters and photographers stood shoulder to shoulder, and I was surprised at the size of the cameras—like telescopes. I realized they would be able to see us during a very private time. Here I thought we would be protected, and we weren't protected at all. Not at all. I felt so vulnerable, so helpless."[1]

Marie's grandparents' property lay adjacent to the cemetery. From behind her grandfather's garage, one Amish man emerged, then another, then another. One by one, over three dozen Amish men and women walked out in a line and created a human shield, crescent-shaped, to hide the gravesite from the reporters and photographers. "Up until then," Marie explained, "the Amish had stayed out of sight. They didn't want to make it worse for us. They had come to attend the burial, to express their compassion and grace.

"We live among the Amish. I knew this was against their foundational beliefs. I had always cringed when I saw tourists taking pictures of the Amish. Here they were standing between us and the media, allowing themselves to be photographed. I had been crying out for God's protection, never dreaming *who* He would send to offer protection. It touched my heart in such a deep way."

The burial lasted about ten to fifteen minutes, and then the Amish took a moment to introduce themselves, one by one, to Marie. "Several parents had lost daughters in the school," Marie said. "It was so overwhelming in many ways. They weren't strangers to us, but now I was face-to-face with a parent whose daughter died because of Charlie's choices. They wanted to show compassion to me."

The immediate, complete, and sincere forgiveness of Charlie's actions by the Amish was powerful. "The Amish were coming to me based on their relationship with God. *That's* what motivated them. They didn't want the spotlight turned on them."

And Marie is quick to turn the spotlight away from her, away even from the Amish, and onto God. "I felt the presence of the Lord in those very first moments, right after I received a phone call from Charlie telling me he wouldn't be coming home again. Healing had already begun. The Lord separated that wall of shame for me from Charlie's actions. The Amish forgave Charlie. And coming so quickly to me took the weight of responsibility off me."

Pain is universal, Marie said. "We all face pain and loss and not always because of our own choices. But the healing of the Lord is available in those places."

Early in her marriage to Charlie, Marie had experienced the loss of two unborn children. "I was always talking to God, trying to grasp His nature. All of those investments came together [on October 2, 2006]. Everything I knew about life was over, but one thing remained: God. I was in a place of desperation. I knew that day would greatly shape my future. I faced a choice—we were going to sink fast . . . or God would make this redeemable."

She chose God. "My life has been flooded with the grace of the Lord. I want to live that grace."

That doesn't mean each day is easy. "What Charlie did, it will forever impact my life and my family's life. But it's not the definition of who I am."

A counselor gave Marie some wise advice. He told her that whenever she thinks about that horrific event, whenever the questions and self-doubt start coming back, to remind herself that she can write a new ending to the story.

The powers of darkness thought they had prevailed on October 2, 2006, at the Nickel Mines schoolhouse. "But that's not the truth," Marie said. "Evil hadn't won. Because of the power of God, I can write a new ending. One of redemption."

REFLECTIONS ON PEACEMAKING

Marie was left alone and abandoned to answer for someone else's actions. How do you think you would have responded had you been in Marie's position?

"The Lord separated that wall of shame for me from Charlie's actions," she said. "The Amish forgave Charlie. And coming so quickly to me took the weight of responsibility off me." What a gift of grace! How does that knowledge expand your view of God's compassion and love?

Has anyone ever stood up on your behalf and advocated for you? How was this a picture of Jesus's perpetual gift of grace?

God doesn't ask us to forgive others because it's the right or moral thing to do. He asks us to forgive others on the basis of a foundational truth—His great love for us.

 Plain *Truth*

One report said that as many as forty Amish came to the burial of Charlie Roberts. Donations flowed in from around the world to the Bart Fire Station—which acted as a conduit for aid—and a committee was set up to manage the funds. The Nickel Mines Accountability Committee designated some of its funds for Marie Roberts Monville and her children.

It Can Wait

Learn from your failures or you will fail to learn.

Amish proverb

Not long after twenty-year-old Chandler Gerber married, someone T-boned his car. Badly injured, Gerber remained in a coma in the hospital for ten days. "The doctors didn't think I'd make it," Gerber said, "but I did." Surprising the doctors, he made a swift and complete recovery. "My wife and I, we thought we had the worst of life out of the way."[1]

Two years later, the day before Gerber turned twenty-two years old, a month before his wife was due to deliver their first child, he was driving to work on S.R. 124, a main road in Adams County, Indiana. It was a sunny April morning and he was texting back and forth with his wife. He typed the words "I love you" and hit the send button.

Gerber was driving the speed limit, about sixty miles per hour, heading east directly into the sunrise. He kept his eyes on his phone to wait for his wife's response. Suddenly, his car hit something and he slammed on the brakes. His mind took in the unfathomable—an Amish buggy had been directly in front of his car. He described an eerie silence, a frozen scene. Small bodies had tumbled out on the ground. The only thing moving was the injured horse. "And in the next moment, it was chaos. Police arrived, traffic gridlocked. I was sobbing as I grasped what I had caused. I knew."

Chandler, he thought to himself as he sat in a friend's car, waiting to be questioned, *be honest. You were being careless. You caused this. You have to take responsibility for this.* "I didn't want to lie. As a follower of Christ, I had to take responsibility for it."

Up to this point in his life, Gerber described his walk of faith as being relatively easy. "It was like God was saying, 'You've talked a good game. When the heat turns up, are you going to turn and run?'"

All six members of the Amish family traveling in the buggy were transported to the hospital. Two children were pronounced dead on arrival; another child died later. The Amish mother was hospitalized with injuries. Gerber was also sent to the hospital to have his blood levels tested for alcohol or drugs, which were negative.

The next day, a police officer met Gerber at his grandparents' house to inform him that an investigation about the accident was under way. "I told the police officer I was texting my wife and he took my phone, recorded my statement," Gerber said. "And then he told me that I could be facing eight years in a federal prison for reckless manslaughter. My heart sank again. Our whole world shook."

Then the police officer did something that stunned Gerber. "Would you mind," the officer said, "if I prayed with you real quick?" The family gathered in a circle to be prayed for by this officer.

Bluffton, Indiana, is a small town. "Everybody knows everybody, or someone who knows someone else," Gerber said. "Soon after the accident, the Amish family I hit sent word that they forgave me, that they knew I didn't mean to cause that accident. I'll never forget that level of forgiveness. They released me, the way God forgives me." He wanted to connect with the family, to let them know how sorry he was, but he was strongly advised by lawyers from the insurance company to not meet with the Amish family. Gerber complied, but grudgingly. "It goes back to the honesty thing. There's only one version. There's one story. I told it to the police. There are not two versions. I'm responsible. I caused this. When I told the lawyer that, he looked at me kind of dazed."

Within weeks, a letter arrived for Gerber from Martin Schwartz, the Amish father who had lost three children in the accident. The following is what he had to say to Gerber:

Dear Ones, trusting in God's ways, how does this find you? Hope all in good health and in good cheer. Around here, we are all on the go and try to make the best we can. I always wonder if we take enough time with our children. Wishing you the best with your little one in the unknown future. I think of you often. Keep looking up, God is always there.

Sincerely,
Martin and Mary
Schwartz

Gerber felt overwhelmed that this Amish couple had concern for him. "It was like he was trying to reassure *me*," Gerber said. "They helped me to heal. Forgiving myself took a long time. A lot of counseling, therapy. But the Amish family, within twenty-four hours, they released me from shame and guilt." He paused and took a deep breath. "Forgiveness can do so much."

The legal ramifications from the accident took over a year to wind their way through the court system. "The prosecutor was in a tough position," Gerber said. "A lot of people in town wanted to throw the book at me, to make a point, an example to others about texting and driving. No matter what he recommended, half the town would be upset. He took it to a grand jury. Within a few hours, they acquitted me. They decided that I had made a mistake, but it wasn't a criminal act."

As soon as Gerber was exonerated, he and his family went straight to meet with the Schwartz family. "Everyone met us out on the porch. They introduced me to everyone, and I was able to tell them that I was going to do everything I could to get the word out to not text and drive. I felt good that I could try to redeem the tragedy. I thought we might stay twenty minutes, but we ended up being there a few hours."

Again, Gerber was astounded by their gracious forgiveness. "I felt so ashamed when I had first heard of their forgiveness of me. I thought of the grudges I held, the things I hold on to. Since then I've vowed to try to never hold grudges. All of us have people who've wronged us, hurt us. It's natural humanness to hold on to things. But their example has challenged me to get to their level of faith. I tell myself, 'Chandler, *what* are you talking about?' It's a constant reminder to release things and forgive. Life is too short to hold on to stuff."

Soon after, out of the blue, Gerber was contacted by Werner Herzog, a world-famous filmmaker known for edgy and memorable documentaries. Herzog asked Gerber if he would participate in a short film called *From One Second to the Next*. AT&T had approached Herzog to create four thirty-second public service announcement commercials for an anti-texting-and-driving "It Can Wait" national ad campaign. Herzog planned to feature four lives that were impacted by texting while driving.

In an NPR interview, Herzog said he wanted to show the interior side of the catastrophes, the suffering and the guilt that never leave. He quickly sensed that the thirty-second PSAs were not enough. "These deep emotions, this inner landscape can only be shown if you have more time. You have to know the persons. You have to allow silences, for example, deep silences of great suffering."[2] Herzog took the four commercials and turned them into a haunting documentary, thirty-five minutes long. It has had over three million views on YouTube and has been distributed to over 40,000 high schools. Gerber's role in both the documentary and the TV spots was particularly emotive because he spoke of his longing regret over texting and driving. It doesn't go away, that kind of sorrow.

Since the documentary aired, Gerber has become a national spokesman about the dangers of texting behind the wheel. Not long ago, Katie Couric invited him as a guest on the *Katie* show. Toward the end of the interview, Gerber told Couric, "I'll never forget. That level of forgiveness is not easy."

Katie Couric leaned forward on her chair. "How? How is that level of forgiveness possible?"

He responded without flinching. "It's only possible with a relationship with Jesus Christ and the power of God's love. It's not possible on our own. No way could that have been possible without Jesus."

That concluding remark, Gerber said, disappointment tingeing his voice, was the only line that was cut from the interview. And yet, he reminded himself, at least the camera crew heard him say it. "I want to be used by God. I want God to bring good from this, to bring good from bad. Had the Amish family not forgiven me, if they were still upset, I couldn't feel comfortable doing this." He paused. "Forgiveness can do so much."

 REFLECTIONS ON PEACEMAKING

Obviously, not texting and driving is Chandler Gerber's main message. There's even more from this powerful story: telling the truth, facing responsibility, asking for and accepting forgiveness. Most people's response would be self-preservation. Denial is an automatic reaction; offering excuses would be natural. But Gerber "owned" his actions that caused this accident. He couldn't contradict his walk as a Christian, despite the consequences. Why is responding with telling the truth much better than self-preservation?

And then, the most important point of all that Gerber makes, asking God to bring good out of a bleak situation. How has God brought redemption from the pain in your life?

Gerber said that the Amish family has challenged his faith to reach a deeper level. What influences have caused your faith in God to increase?

Plain *Truth*

The horse and buggy is the most defining aspect of Amish identity. It's their symbol, their icon. A continual reminder that they are separate from the world. So why have they rejected the automobile? In a word: limitation. A horse and buggy can travel about fifteen miles, so most church members live within that radius. They believe that horse-drawn transportation holds communities together by slowing the pace and limiting mobility.

And yet Amish buggies are frequently involved in road accidents. Crashes happen more often at night and in many cases involve drivers under the influence. Amish are often killed or seriously hurt, as are their horses, which may have to be put down after accidents. Still, the Amish hold tight to this tradition. John H., an Amish farmer in Independence, Iowa, said, "I believe the reason we have survived all these years, unlike others [like the nearby Amana Colonies], is because we don't have cars. We stay close together."

Honoring a Parent Who Is Not Honorable

Contentment is not getting what we want but being satisfied with what we have.

Amish proverb

A teapot is whistling on an iron cookstove in a kitchen so spartan there is no sink, only a long countertop. This is the home of an Old Order Amish family, belonging to a church so conservative that running water, all indoor plumbing, is not permitted. On the countertop is an assortment of dishes and utensils and a world globe—something that seems oddly out of place in a modest Amish farmhouse. It's placed close enough to grab for quick references. The spring day is gray and rainy and cold, but there is warmth in this house. Kindness and love. Things that Anne M. wouldn't have found in her childhood home.

Anne never heard an "I love you" from her father. While that might seem harsh to modern ears, it's not an uncommon thing for those of stoic German heritage. Another Amish friend once remarked that while she never heard those words, she never doubted her parents loved her.

Anne, a quiet, reflective, fortysomething woman, never felt her father loved her. The words she did hear were not affirming ones. "My father never once struck me," she said, "but he also never said a kind word." He said words that could never be forgotten. Words she would carry with her for the rest of her life. Words that made the road to forgiveness a long one to travel.

Anne described her father as a merciless man, who controlled the family with his piercing gaze that swept over everyone and found them lacking. She remembered a lifetime of lessons and lectures. Of mollifying him. "Growing up, it felt like walking on eggshells, all the time. You didn't want to set Dad off."

If her father found chores undone, they would never hear the end of it. "He was particularly hard on the boys. Scolding them for the smallest infraction. Forgetting to put away a halter, leaving a tool out in the yard. He would berate and belittle us, calling us names. There were only two ways to do things: Dad's way and the wrong way. I remember a time when something made Dad mad and he took it out on my oldest brother—calling him stupid and lazy and worthless. My brother broke down—a twelve-year-old, sobbing like a baby."

Did Anne love her father? She took her time answering, gathering her words carefully. "We children loved him at a distance. Mostly, we feared him. It always made me cringe when the preacher would speak about the Ten Commandments. You know, the one with the promise."

She's referring to Exodus 20:12, the fifth of the Ten Commandments, that says, "Honor your father and your mother," then adds, "so that you may live long in the land the LORD your God is giving you." Paul notes in Ephesians 6:2 that it's the first commandment with a promise attached to it. But how do you honor a parent who isn't honorable?

Honoring your parents is at the core of being a follower of Christ, because it means that we are thankful to God for the very life He has given us. Honoring a parent—even a parent who is dishonorable—means *not* rejecting the story God has put you in, and believing that God is working *in* that story.

This doesn't mean you're grateful for everything, but it doesn't mean you aren't grateful for *anything*. Gratitude allows us to be thankful for who a person is, to stop demanding satisfaction and perfection all the time. Gratitude, states a Harvard Health Publication, is the healthiest emotion of all. "In positive psychology research, gratitude is strongly and consistently associated with greater happiness. Gratitude helps people feel more positive emotions, relish good experiences, improve their health, deal with adversity, and build strong relationships. Most studies published on this topic have found an association between gratitude and an individual's well-being."[1]

Interestingly, the word *gratitude* is derived from the Latin word *gratia*, which means grace, graciousness, or gratefulness. In some ways gratitude encompasses all of these meanings.

Certainly, there are some situations when grace for the past can be extended, but limited contact with a toxic parent is essential. One friend, whose father sexually abused her and whose mother not only denied it but was furious with her daughter for confronting the abuse, had to limit involvement with her parents after she had children of her own. She sends holiday and birthday cards to her parents, wishing them well and acknowledging their good qualities, thanking them for past blessings. It might seem a small gesture, but she's found a way to honor them from afar and still protect herself and her children. Yes, it might seem a small and simple gesture . . . but it's really quite an extraordinary one, with returning benefits.

Dr. Martin E. P. Seligman, a leading researcher and psychologist at the University of Pennsylvania, tested the impact of various positive psychology interventions on 411 people, each compared with a control assignment of writing about early memories. When their week's assignment was to write and personally deliver a letter of gratitude to someone who had never been properly thanked for his or her kindness, participants immediately exhibited a huge increase in happiness scores. This impact was greater than that from any other intervention, with benefits lasting for a month.[2] Imagine that—your well-being *receives* benefits, lasting a month, by *giving* thanks.

So it seems that an essential part of coming to peace with a dishonorable parent is to separate out the good qualities from the bad ones. And in most cases, there are some good qualities.

As Anne shared about her father on that rainy spring morning, she reminisced about good times too. Her father liked to travel. He planned trips each year for the family to see the national parks. He had an insatiable curiosity about the world. "Dad visited forty-seven states," she said, a trace of pride in her voice. "He wanted to see all fifty, but the cancer interrupted that." It turns out the world globe in her kitchen had belonged to him. It seemed he passed his curiosity about the world on to his daughter.

Anne's father died two years ago. She left her family to return to her father's home and help nurse him through his final days. The day before he passed, she had a last, healing talk with her father. Lying on his deathbed, was he at all remorseful? Had his heart softened? Did he tell her that he loved her? She never elaborated on what had been communicated between them. But she lifted her eyes and gave a gentle smile, and it was like a cloud had moved past the sun, spilling light into the kitchen. "It all ended well," she said.

And isn't that what our aim should be in our journey of life? To end well.

 REFLECTIONS ON PEACEMAKING

We cannot be thankful for who we are without being thankful for our parents, through whom our life came. They are a part of our identity. It's possible to acknowledge the flaws of a parent and still discover ways to honor that parent—to will and to work for good in their life. What are some ways that you "will and work for good" in your parents' lives?

Anne M. said her story with her father "ended well." She didn't elaborate on what that meant, but it's possible that her story ended well *not* because her father's heart had softened but because she had done all she could to reconcile their relationship. She had fulfilled her responsibility (Rom. 12:18). Only God can change someone's heart. But that doesn't mean you can't end your side of the story well. What needs to happen in your life so that you can make sure your story ends well? Gratitude and forgiveness can lead to a good ending to a story.

 Plain *Truth*

"Recent research on the health benefits of forgiveness shows that people who can make this mental shift may benefit in ways they didn't anticipate—namely, by living longer. In a study aptly called 'Forgive to Live,' Luther College psychologist Loren Toussaint and colleagues investigated the relationships among forgiveness, religiousness, spirituality, health, and mortality in a national U.S. sample of 1500 adults age 66 and older. The study, published in the *Journal of Behavioral Medicine*, was the first to test the benefits of forgiveness to a long life. . . . To sum it up, if you want to benefit from the life-extending benefits of forgiveness, don't wait for others to apologize to you or to promise that they will change. Start the process within your own mind, and you'll be happier, and live longer."[3]

Epilogue

One summer, my seventy-four-year-old sharp-as-a-tack father started to show signs of tip-of-the-tongue-itis. It was a change in my dad, but everyone struggles to capture a word now and then. It didn't seem like the red flag for early stage Alzheimer's disease that it was.

Later that year, another red flag went up, far more worrisome. Dad's judgment. A phone call from Canada came in to my dad to inform him that he had won a sweepstakes worth millions of dollars. The money was waiting for him in US Customs, as soon as he sent a five thousand dollar fee, via any Western Union telegraph office, to clear the winnings through customs. The caller ended the call with a cheery "God bless you!"

My younger brother found a pile of Western Union telegraphs in Dad's office. Apparently Dad had been sending customs fees via Western Union . . . over and over again. The callers were con artists, scammers. They would sell his name to another con artist, so the calls kept on coming, Dad kept on hoping, and he kept on sending his money through Western Union.

As soon as my brother found those telegraphs and alerted the family, we dropped a net around our parents' finances. We changed their telephone number, contacted the police and the FBI (no help there), closed bank accounts (we discovered fraudulent activity), and got Dad to the doctor for an accurate diagnosis.

In total, Dad had been scammed out of one hundred thirty-five thousand dollars. *From the equity line on their house.*

The combination of the Alzheimer's diagnosis and the financial crisis created by the con artists forced my parents to sell their home of thirty years. Thus began a long, sad decline into dementia for my dad.

These con artists have never been found. They are probably still at it, scamming other vulnerable elderly people. I'm not sure why—perhaps because they were nameless and faceless—but it was never hard for me to forgive them. Instead of spending time and energy trying to recover the lost money, attention was better spent focused on the rapidly changing needs of my parents.

The benefits of forgiveness are very appealing, but what motivates me to forgive is more important. I felt an assurance that the crimes of those con artists did not go unnoticed by God. Throughout Scripture is a theme that God cares deeply about the vulnerable—people like my dad. Leaving the comeuppance of those con artists in the hands of God, who is wise and just and good, was deeply satisfying to me. It relieved me of the need for revenge. Proverbs 20:22 was helpful: "Do not say, 'I'll pay you back for this wrong!' Wait for the LORD, and he will avenge you."

And that's exactly what He did. A miracle started to unfold in my parents' dismal financial situation.

After their house was sold, my parents moved into an assisted living facility. In our haste, most of their belongings were packed in a storage unit to be dealt with later. Little by little, my sister and I weeded out the storage unit.

One day in late June, after another storage unit cleanout session, I brought home a carload of my parents' belongings to sort through. Now, by nature, I am a tosser-outer. There was a box of papers that I had shoved to a corner to be tossed in the weekly recycling bin for garbage pickup. My husband, a much more thorough and detailed person than I am, spent the fourth of July—a particularly hot day—carefully going through that box, making sure there were no Social Security numbers or any identifying information, just to ensure my parents' protection.

In that dusty, moldy box, my husband found some long-forgotten stock certificates. He gave them to my older brother, who then went through the painstaking process of determining the original sales price, locating the broker, and finding out if the stock certificates still held any value.

A few months later, my brother called to say that he had a final count on the value of those forgotten stock certificates. Are you sitting down? They were worth over one hundred thirty-five thousand dollars. The *same* amount of money that the Canadian Sweepstakes con artists had scammed from my dad. Amazing!

There were so many spiritual realities that were displayed in this experience with my dad and the con artists—but the biggest lesson was about trusting God. We can hand over to God our wounds and worries, grudges and battle scars, trusting that He will see us through to the end. "The LORD is my strength and my shield, my heart trusts in him and he helps me. My heart leaps for joy, and with my song I praise him" (Ps. 28:7).

The truth about forgiveness is that it all flows from God. It is not in our nature to forgive. It is God's nature, His business, and it is only by God's equipping that we can forgive others. Only God.

Anglican preacher and evangelical leader John Stott wrote, "Our calling is not to conformity to the world around us but to a radical nonconformity."[1] What, truly, could be a more radical nonconformity than displaying authentic forgiveness in our daily life? God wants to free, encourage, and heal your heart so that your story ends well. Will you let Him? Ask and you shall receive (Matt. 7:7–8). *That* is a promise.

Notes

Introduction

1. Donald B. Kraybill, Steven M. Nolt, and David L. Weaver-Zercher, *Amish Grace: How Forgiveness Transcended Tragedy* (San Francisco: John Wiley & Sons, 2007), 52.
2. John Stott, *Through the Bible, Through the Year* (Grand Rapids: Baker, 2011), 74.
3. Dick Tibbits with Steve Halliday, *Forgive to Live: How Forgiveness Can Save Your Life* (Franklin, TN: Integrity, 2006), 166.
4. *The Papers of Martin Luther King, Jr.*, vol. 6 (Berkeley and Los Angeles: University of California Press, 2007), 488.

Everyday Friction

1. "Brain Trivia," *Education*, Laboratory of Neuro Imaging, University of Southern California, http://www.loni.usc.edu/about_loni/education/brain_trivia.php.
2. Daniel Kahneman, "How Do Experiences Become Memories?" NPR radio, May 24, 2013, http://www.wbur.org/npr/182676143/how-do-experiences-become-memories.

A Little Amish General Store

1. Brené Brown, *Daring Greatly* (New York: Gotham Books, 2012), 171.
2. "Amish Population by State (2014)," Young Center for Anabaptist and Pietist Studies, Elizabethtown College, http://www2.etown.edu/amishstudies/Population_by_State_2014.asp.

The Red Mutza

1. The story of the red Mutza was originally retold in a letter written by a descendant of Bishop Mose.

2. Ken Sande and Kevin Johnson, *Resolving Everyday Conflict* (Grand Rapids: Baker, 2011), 21–22.

3. John Hostetler, *Amish Society* (Baltimore: The Johns Hopkins University Press, 1993), 239–40.

A Jar of Pickles

1. Sande and Johnson, *Resolving Everyday Conflict*, 36–37.

2. "Why Don't Amish Sue?" *Amish America* blog, August 23, 2012, http://amishamerica.com/why-dont-amish-sue/.

Three Words a Mother Never Wants to Hear from Her Fifteen-Year-Old Daughter

1. Brené Brown, "The Power of Vulnerability," TED Talk, June 2010, Houston, http://www.ted.com/talks/brene_brown_on_vulnerability.

2. "Frequently Asked Questions," Amish Studies, Young Center for Anabaptist and Pietist Studies, Elizabethtown College, http://www2.etown.edu/amishstudies/FAQ.asp.

Keeping Secrets

1. Sande and Johnson, *Resolving Everyday Conflict*, 62.

2. Dietrich Bonhoeffer, *Life Together: The Classic Exploration of Faith in Community* (New York: Harper, 1954), 112–13.

3. Ibid., 116–17.

4. Max Lucado, "When You Become the Thing You Hate," *Family Life* magazine, http://www.familylife.com/articles/topics/faith/essentials/repentance/when-you-become-the-thing-you-hate#.U6ioYI1dXQk.

5. Donald B. Kraybill, Karen M. Johnson-Weiner, and Steven M. Nolt, *The Amish* (Baltimore: The Johns Hopkins University Press, 2013), 92–93.

When Parents Make Mistakes

1. "Frequently Asked Questions," Amish Studies, http://www2.etown.edu/amishstudies/FAQ.asp.

Friendly Fire

1. Ken Sande, phone interview with author, November 2012.

2. http://christian-quotes.ochristian.com/Harry-Ironside-Quotes/.

3. Andrew Clouse, "What Is an Anabaptist Christian?" *Mennonite Mission Network* blog, February 18, 2013, http://www.mennonitemission .net/Stories/BeyondOurselves/AnabaptistChristian/Pages/WhatisanAna baptistChristian.aspx.

It's Never about the Furniture

1. Gary Inrig, *The Risk of Forgiveness: What It Means to Forgive* (Grand Rapids: RBC Ministries, 2013), 13–14.
2. Mark McMinn, *Why Sin Matters* (Wheaton: Tyndale, 2004), 161.
3. Inrig, *Risk of Forgiveness*, 12.
4. Ibid., 27.
5. C. S. Lewis, *Letters to Malcolm, Chiefly on Prayer* (San Diego: Harcourt, 1991), 27.
6. Donald B. Kraybill, Steven M. Nolt, and David L. Weaver-Zercher, *The Amish Way: Patient Faith in a Perilous World* (San Francisco: Jossey-Bass, 2010), 348–49.

Make Your Stuff

1. Joe Wittmer, phone interview with author, March 13, 2012.

The Stories We Tell Our Children

1. James W. Lowry, *The Martyrs' Mirror Made Plain: How to Study and Profit from the Martyrs' Mirror* (Almyer, ON: Pathway Publishers, 2000), 112–13.
2. Kraybill, Nolt, and Weaver-Zercher, *Amish Grace*, 70.

A Turned Cheek and a Loaf of Bread

1. Mary Ann Kinsinger, phone interview with author, May 2, 2014.
2. Hostetler, *Amish Society*, 63.

Inside the Ring of Protection

1. Patricia Yollin, "Mt. Vision Fire: 10 Years After," *SFGate*, October 2, 2005, http://www.sfgate.com/bayarea/article/MOUNT-VISION-FIRE-10-Years-After-Once-ravaged-2604520.php.
2. Donald B. Kraybill, *The Puzzles of Amish Life*, rev. ed. (Intercourse, PA: Good Books, 1998), 32, 34.

Turning Points

1. Wilma L. Derksen, phone interview with author, April 30, 2014.
2. Tibbits, *Forgive to Live*, 166.

3. John Piper, "Forgive Us Our Debtors," sermon, Bethlehem Baptist Church, Minneapolis, MN, March 20, 1994, http://www.desiringgod.org/sermons/as-we-forgive-our-debtors.

The Unthinkable

1. Wilma L. Derksen, *Have You Seen Candace? A Mother's True Story of Coping with the Murder of Her Daughter* (Winnipeg: Amity Publishers, 2011), 30.
2. Ibid.
3. Wilma L. Derksen, phone interview with author, April 30, 2014. Subsequent quotes are from the author's interview with Wilma unless noted otherwise.
4. Derksen, *Have You Seen Candace?*, 224.

Twist of Faith

1. Anne Beiler, speech, 2012 Forgiveness Conference held at The Family Center, Gap, Pennsylvania, October 6, 2012.
2. Jonas Beiler, speech, 2012 Forgiveness Conference held at The Family Center, Gap, Pennsylvania, October 6, 2012.
3. Jonas Beiler with Shawn Smucker, *Think No Evil* (New York: Howard Books, 2009), 125.
4. Ibid., 180.

Stuck in Bed

1. A. H. Harris et al., "Effects of a Group Forgiveness Intervention on Forgiveness, Perceived Stress and Trait Anger: A Randomized Trial," *Journal of Clinical Psychology* 62, no. 6 (2006): 715–33, http://learningtoforgive.com/research/effects-of-group-forgiveness-intervention-on-perceived-stress-state-and-trait-anger-symptoms-of-stress-self-reported-health-and-forgiveness-stanford-forgiveness-project/. The study comes from Luskin's work; Fred Luskin, *Forgive for Good* (San Francisco: HarperOne, 2003).
2. Loren Toussaint, Amy D. Owen, and Alyssa Cheadle, "Forgive to Live: Forgiveness, Health, and Longevity," *Journal of Behavioral Medicine* 35, no. 4 (August 2012): 375–86, http://link.springer.com/article/10.1007/s10865-011-9362-4.
3. Tibbits, *Forgive to Live*, 9, 68.
4. Bryan Bell, *Lessons in Lifemanship* blog, http://bbll.com/ch10.html.
5. Hostetler, *Amish Society*, 170.

The Sugarcreek Scandal

1. "Amish Man Gets 6½ Years in $17M, Multi-State Fraud Case," Money, *USA Today*, June 13, 2012, http://usatoday30.usatoday.com/money /economy/story/2012-06-13/amish-man-ohio-scam/55580638/1.

2. Diana B. Henriques, "Broken Trust in God's Country," *New York Times*, February 25, 2012, http://www.nytimes.com/2012/02/26/business /in-amish-country-accusations-of-a-ponzi-scheme.html?pagewanted=all &_r=0.

3. Kraybill, Nolt, and Weaver-Zercher, *Amish Grace*, 182.

4. Frederick Buechner, *Wishful Thinking: A Seeker's ABC* (New York: Harper & Row, 1973), 29.

5. Erik Wesner, "Figuring Out Success with the Amish," *The High Calling*, May 27, 2014, http://www.thehighcalling.org/7394/figuring-out -success-with-the-amish#.U7xqiY1dXig.

Blessing Our Circumstances

1. Sherry Gore, phone interview with author, May 2013.

A Four-Hundred-Year-Old Bible

1. Quotes are taken from Sabine Aschmann, email correspondence with author, February 2014.

2. Joanne Hess Siegrist, interview with Lloyd Hoover, founder of Muddy Creek Farm Library, Ephrata, Pennsylvania.

Through My Tears

1. Becki Reiser and Michael Comella, *Through My Tears: Awash in Forgiveness* (Becki Reiser, 2014), 306.

2. Ibid., 296.

3. Ibid.

4. Ibid.

5. Kraybill, Nolt, and Weaver-Zercher, *Amish Way*, 155.

Rachel's Stand

1. Inrig, *Risk of Forgiveness*, 26.

2. Tibbits, *Forgive to Live*, 171.

3. Beth Moore, *Breaking Free: Discover the Victory of Total Surrender* (Nashville: B&H, 2007), 106.

4. Kraybill, *Puzzles of Amish Life*, 32.

Grace Walked In

1. Kraybill, Nolt, and Weaver-Zercher, *Amish Way*, xi.

Two Lives

1. Terri Roberts, phone interview with author, May 2014. Terri's full story will be told in her forthcoming book *Forgiven: The Amish School Shooting, a Mother's Love, and a Story of Remarkable Grace*, available Fall 2015 from Bethany House Publishers, a division of Baker Publishing Group.

2. Kraybill, Nolt, and Weaver-Zercher, *Amish Grace*, 94–95.

Shielding Marie

1. Marie Roberts Monville, phone interview with author, February 2014.

It Can Wait

1. Chandler Gerber, phone interview with author, June 2014.

2. Werner Herzog, "Herzog Plumbs Guilt and Loss Wrought by Texting and Driving," NPR radio interview, August 16, 2013, http://www .npr.org/blogs/alltechconsidered/2013/08/16/212337606/herzog-plumbs -guilt-and-loss-wrought-by-texting-and-driving.

Honoring a Parent Who Is Not Honorable

1. "In Praise of Gratitude," *Harvard Health Publications*, Harvard Medical School, November 2011, http://www.health.harvard.edu/newsletters/ Harvard_Mental_Health_Letter/2011/November/in-praise-of-gratitude.

2. M. E. P. Seligman et al., "Empirical Validation of Interventions," *American Psychologist* 60, no. 1 (July–August 2005): 410–21.

3. Susan Krauss Whitbourne, "Fulfillment at Any Age: Living Longer by Practicing Forgiveness," *Psychology Today*, January 1, 2013, http:// www.psychologytoday.com/blog/fulfillment-any-age/201301/live-longer -practicing-forgiveness.

Epilogue

1. Stott, *Through the Bible*, 74.

Recommended Reading

There are many excellent books about the Amish. The following list provides accurate sources to give the reader a greater understanding of the Amish and their culture. Those listed here represent my personal recommendations.

Hostetler, John. *Amish Society*. Baltimore: The Johns Hopkins University Press, 1993.

Kraybill, Donald B. *The Puzzles of Amish Life*, rev. ed. Intercourse, PA: Good Books, 1998.

Kraybill, Donald B., Steven M. Nolt, and David L. Weaver-Zercher. *Amish Grace: How Forgiveness Transcended Tragedy*. San Francisco: John Wiley & Sons, 2007.

Wittmer, Joe. *The Gentle People: An Inside View of Amish Life*. Washington, IN: Black Buggy, 2007.

Recommended books about forgiveness:

Beiler, Jonas, with Shawn Smucker. *Think No Evil*. New York: Howard Books, 2009.

Derksen, Wilma L. *Have You Seen Candace? A Mother's True Story of Coping with the Murder of Her Daughter*. Winnipeg: Amity Publishers, 2011.

Inrig, Gary. *The Risk of Forgiveness: What It Means to Forgive.* Grand Rapids: RBC Ministries, 2013.

Luskin, Fred. *Forgive for Good.* San Francisco: HarperOne, 2003.

McMinn, Mark R. *Why Sin Matters.* Wheaton: Tyndale, 2004.

Monville, Marie, with Cindy Lambert. *One Light Still Shines.* Grand Rapids: Zondervan, 2013.

Reiser, Becki, and Michael Comella. *Through My Tears: Awash in Forgiveness.* Becki Reiser, 2014.

Sande, Ken, and Kevin Johnson. *Resolving Everyday Conflict.* Grand Rapids: Baker, 2011.

Sittser, Gerald L. *A Grace Disguised: How the Soul Grows through Loss.* Grand Rapids: Zondervan, 1996.

Smedes, Lewis. *Forgive and Forget.* San Francisco: HarperCollins, 1984.

Tibbits, Dick, with Steve Halliday. *Forgive to Live: How Forgiveness Can Save Your Life.* Franklin, TN: Integrity, 2006.

Tutu, Desmond. *No Future without Forgiveness.* New York: Doubleday, 2000.

Suzanne Woods Fisher is the author of the bestselling Lancaster County Secrets and Stoney Ridge Seasons series. *The Search* received a 2012 Carol Award, *The Waiting* was a finalist for the 2011 Christy Award, and *The Choice* was a finalist for the 2011 Carol Award. Suzanne's grandfather was raised in the Old Order German Baptist Brethren Church in Franklin County, Pennsylvania. Her interest in living a simple, faith-filled life began with her Dunkard cousins. Suzanne is also the author of the bestselling *Amish Peace: Simple Wisdom for a Complicated World* and *Amish Proverbs: Words of Wisdom from the Simple Life*, both finalists for the ECPA Book of the Year award, and *Amish Values for Your Family: What We Can Learn from the Simple Life*. She has an app, Amish Wisdom, to deliver a proverb a day to your iPhone, iPad, or Android. Visit her at www.suzannewoodsfisher.com to find out more.

Suzanne lives with her family in the San Francisco Bay Area.

Meet Suzanne online at

 Suzanne Woods Fisher

suzannewfisher

www.SuzanneWoodsFisher.com

Download the
Free **Amish Wisdom** App

Make the Peace and Wisdom of the Amish a Reality in Your Life

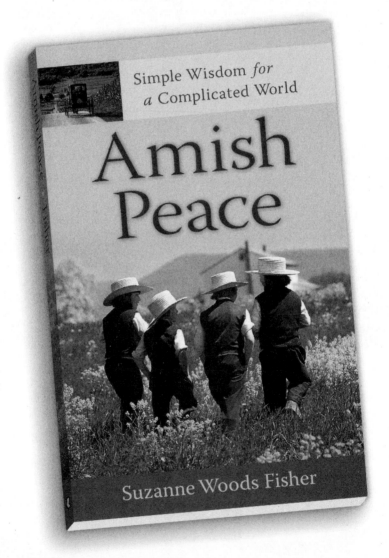

Simple Wisdom *for* *a* Complicated World

Amish Peace

Suzanne Woods Fisher

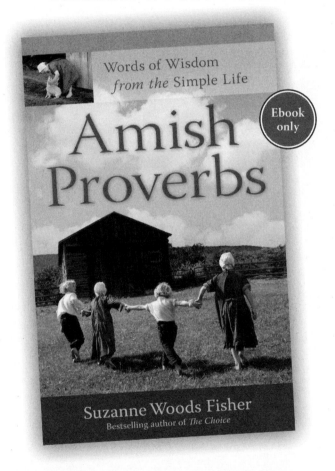

Values like community, forgiveness, simple living, obedience, and more can be your family legacy— without selling your car, changing your wardrobe, or moving out to farm country.

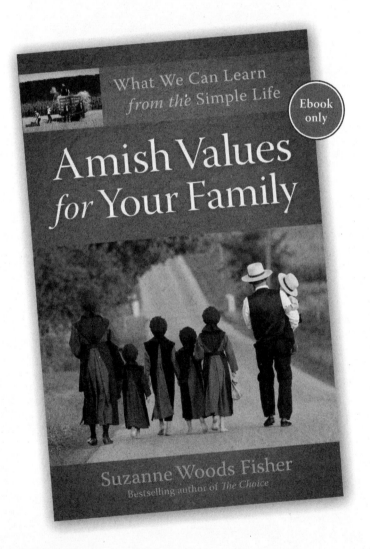

What We Can Learn *from the* Simple Life

Ebook only

Amish Values *for* Your Family

Suzanne Woods Fisher

Bestselling author of *The Choice*

"Everything I love in a novel . . .
Fast paced, character driven, filled with
rich descriptions and enjoyable dialogue."
—SHELLEY SHEPARD GRAY,
New York Times and *USA Today* bestselling author

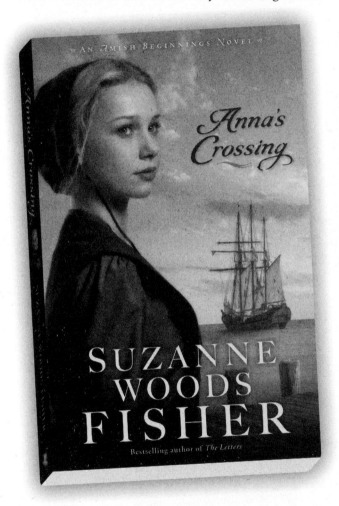

Suzanne Woods Fisher invites you back to the beginning of Amish life
in America with this fascinating glimpse into the first ocean crossing—
and the lives of two intrepid people who braved it.

WELCOME TO A PLACE OF UNCONDITIONAL LOVE AND UNEXPECTED BLESSINGS

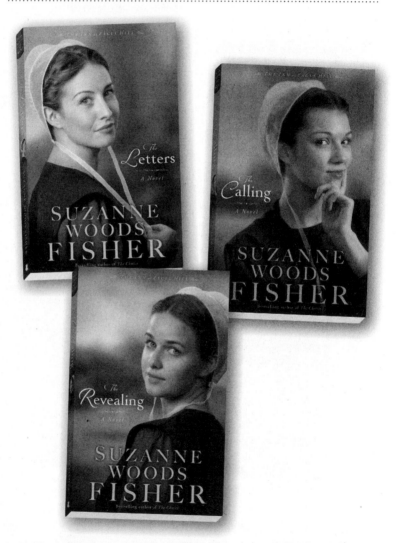

Don't miss the Stoney Ridge Seasons series!

DON'T MISS THE
LANCASTER COUNTY *Secrets* SERIES!

Every day is a *new adventure!*

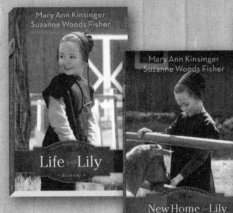

For children ages 8–12

For a child, every day is a thing of wonder. And for young Lily Lapp, every day is a new opportunity for blessings, laughter, family, and a touch of mischief.

AdventuresofLilyLapp.com